The Birdman

# The Birdman

*Memories of birds by*
HENRY DOUGLAS-HOME

*With a Foreword by*
THE LORD HOME OF THE HIRSEL

*Edited by* JOHN MCEWEN

*Line drawings by*
SIR PETER SCOTT AND ROBERT GILLMOR

READERS UNION
Group of Book Clubs
*Newton Abbot*

First published by Collins, 1977
Reprinted 1978

© in the text Henry Douglas-Home

© in the line drawings Sir Peter Scott
and Robert Gillmor

ISBN 0 00 219014–1

Printed in Great Britain by
Morrison & Gibb Ltd., London and Edinburgh

*For Peregrine*

# Contents

# List of Plates

# Foreword

This book by my brother Henry is essentially the story of the birds to be found in the Border Country and more particularly in the valleys and woods of The Hirsel which is our home. He has plenty of scope, for since the beginning of the century about a hundred different species have been recorded as nesting in the area, with many more as visitors. He also writes about the large number of species which he has encountered overseas and elsewhere in Britain, and he does it with both the freshness and humour of the amateur and the knowledge of the professional.

Henry is probably best known to most people as a broadcaster. At this he was expert; I remember that when he used to wire the lakeside and the rhododendrons for a contest between Hirsel and Hever in Kent, to see who could broadcast the greatest variety of birdsong, there was never more than one or two in it either way.

The secret of birdwatching is patience, the ability to be quiet, and application to detail. Henry has these qualities in full measure. I recall that, as a young boy, he counted the feathers in the nest of a long-tailed tit and arrived at the total of three thousand three hundred and eighty-three. Recently, I had carelessly labelled a bird as a dunlin but with microscopic attention he proved it to be an immature curlew sandpiper.

One of the most enthralling chapters is that on the habits of the swift. By contriving the right type of nesting-box, with an entrance small enough to exclude the house sparrows, Henry attracted many pairs to the window-sills of The Hirsel and one of these, having wintered in South Africa, returned for fourteen consecutive years. The distance travelled by some of these swifts during their lifetime must be more than three million miles.

## Foreword

A hobby is a splendid thing for the young and, once acquired, it is never lost. Because of the pleasure, information and amusement this book affords, it will surely recruit many new enthusiasts into the field of ornithology.

*Home*

THE LORD HOME OF THE HIRSEL, K.T.

# Author's Preface

In this personal ramble through more than sixty years of memories of birds I am indebted to many people. Two, in particular, deserve mention: my brother Alec for his generous foreword (which luckily left a lot unsaid); and Peter Scott, whose busy life has been dedicated to Nature but who has found time in his arduous schedule to draw some of his superb sketches for me. To him, especially, I owe a great deal – not only for the drawings but also for the knowledge and instruction I have borrowed from him over many years.

I write this preface, in July 1977, in some sorrow. There is no doubt that even in this slight survey of my own experience there looms a mass of evidence of human guilt which no jury could ignore. Humans cannot impress on or control the disorders that Nature decrees – ice ages, droughts in the Sahara, and so on. But the same cannot be said of some of our modern technical efforts to improve the lot of man, which have been made with little consideration for those fellow creatures who had already lived for so many millions of years before we developed our supremacy of mind. Before it is too late we must realise that we hold the keys of destruction – not only of ourselves but also of the more ancient occupants of that world.

During the summer of 1977 I have seen fewer summer visitors than at any time since 1916 when I began making records. Things are no better at the other end of the chain. When my friend Jack Vincent from Natal came on a visit he told me that, during the winter of 1976 he had never seen or heard such a dearth of

European birds: no willow or Garden Warblers, no Sandpipers nor many others.

There are two main causes of their sad decline. First: in this country we are heedlessly changing the habitats of birds (through forestry, hedge removal etc.) but above all we are adding poison to the countryside. We should remember that poison for agricultural increase of yield brought Peregrines to the verge of extinction in North America as their prey became more and more contaminated. Second, but of equal importance: there is mass slaughter of migratory birds each autumn in southern Europe by the use of modern implements like mist-nets and other devices.

The annual loss of so many millions cannot be allowed.

Extinction of a species – animal, bird or fish – is unavoidable if Nature decides that its end is due, but in our recently assumed supremacy we have been guilty of awarding the death sentence to others besides the Dodo, Moa, and Great Auk.

Finally, I would like to end this preface by expressing my gratitude to Johnny McEwen who has spent so many hours and much of his patience trying to translate my thoughts into what we hope may be a readable volume.

HENRY DOUGLAS-HOME
July 21, 1977

# 1. | Introduction

The Hirsel estate lies to the northwest of the famous Scottish border town of Coldstream. Its situation is of great general interest; the land being heavily but beautifully timbered with trees of all ages and enriched by two rivers – the Tweed on its southern boundary and the little Leet –, a twenty-seven acre lake and the occasional presence, when work permits, of an ex-Prime Minister in the form of my eldest brother Alec. But for those who love birds, like myself, it has the additional charm of being an ornithological paradise. Every summer it supports over ninety breeding species and, lying in the path of the great seasonal migrations from Africa and the Arctic, its sheltered woods and waters offer a brief resting place for many more. Owing partly to the enormous increase of public interest in birds and partly to my own attentions over the last sixty years as an amateur ornithologist, broadcaster and lecturer, Hirsel today has become something of a birdwatcher's Mecca. These and other things are the story of this book.

My father was not all that interested in birds but, presumably having recognised my innate enthusiasm for them, in 1916 he sent me a diary from the War front in the Near East with instructions that I should make a daily record in it of all the birds I saw at Hirsel. This I did, further encouraged by weekly accounts of the birds he was seeing in Gallipoli and Mesopotamia, and I have kept it up, with one or two forced interruptions, ever since. That was the start. Unluckily I was short-sighted. Perhaps to compensate my hearing was correspondingly acute and this forced me from the outset to identify birds by their calls rather than their appearance, a more reliable way in any case.

In 1917 I followed Alec to Ludgrove, a preparatory school near New Barnet where there were some keen ornithologists on the staff, especially Mr Stanborough, Mr Brown and Mr Blore, who further educated me in the ways of birds. No pets were allowed at the school – a sensible precaution because few children can spare the time to look after them – but there were nesting boxes in the grounds and several species that we did not get at Hirsel, in particular nuthatches and the tiny lesser spotted woodpecker. Then I went to Eton, and on arrival soon found myself moving once more in ornithological circles, going on expeditions and having my eyes opened to the presence of further novelties – shrikes, reed and marsh warblers, and the astonishing numbers of swifts and cuckoos that are attracted to that part of the Thames Valley. This was 1921 and by then my father had at last returned from the War, having been delayed by the troubles in Ireland where he commanded the Lanarkshire Yeomanry.

It might have been thought that our family was complete. Five of us had emerged by 1914; Alec, Bridget, myself in 1907, Rachel and William. But now with the reappearance of my father, apparently fully refreshed, two more brothers were born: Edward in 1920 and, in 1922, the baby of the family, George. One hesitates to think how many of us there might have been had not the Kaiser intervene!

All of us, even my sisters who are both expert fishers, came into this world more or less with a gun or rod in our hand, and enthusiasm for country pleasures and a delight in the countryside have remained a perpetual bond between us ever since. It is my experience that sportsmen of all kinds are usually the best naturalists and conservationists. They admire nature and try to live in harmony with its mysteries.

Much of the credit for my family's interest in such things must go to my extremely tolerant though attentive parents. My father was always very solicitous of my mother's health and she in turn of ours.

'Poor old Lil,' he would say to us, 'poor old Lil, she's very delicate'. And he refused her permission to ride, although she was a wonderful horsewoman and as tough as anything, living well into her eighties; while she in her turn insisted that we wrap three sheets of *The Times* next to our skin every time we made a journey of over forty miles (the distance from Hirsel to Edinburgh), a practice she noisily maintained throughout her life.

'But Mama is this necessary?' we protested.

'It may not be when you go out from school' she would insist, 'but it's absolutely necessary for the journey. If you don't wear newspaper you're bound to be sick on the train!'

None of us had ever thought of being sick on a train and Collingwood, the butler subsequently enshrined in my brother William's plays, used hurriedly to unwrap us of our embarrassment on the way to the station. As for my father, his life was dedicated to good works and voluntary service. He was a lay preacher and I often accompanied him when he addressed the congregations of the various denominations in Scotland on general pacific themes. He was also quite an eccentric. His father had forbidden him a cheque book for fear of its encouraging youthful extravagance and as a result he remained quite ignorant of their purpose, despite acting as the Governor of the British Linen Bank for thirty years. For cash he had to make do with a weekly allowance of five £1 notes sent in a brown envelope by the family lawyers in Edinburgh. When he came south to take us out from school the amount was raised to £50, which inevitably proved quite inadequate to the demands of a week in London. He used to arrive in Eton at the weekend completely broke, having been far too frightened to call Edinburgh for aid, so that instead of receiving a long-awaited tip we had to bail him out with the remains of our pocket money.

One day after the Second War, when he was old and I was at Scottish Command, I was very disturbed by how ill he suddenly seemed. He hated the thought of a doctor so I persuaded a medical friend of mine, Sir Stanley Davidson, to come down for the weekend to make an assessment on the pretext of being a fishing guest. Much to my surprise Father met us at the door, filled us to overflowing with drink at dinner and entertained us with a series of wonderful memories far past the hour of his normal bed-time.

'Look' said Stanley after my father had eventually retired, 'you've got me here on false pretences. He's the fittest thing I've ever seen!'

However, true to form, Stanley appeared punctually at breakfast next morning, togged up for a day on the river. To his astonishment my father was already halfway through a plate of porridge, reading the paper.

'Sorry. Desperate day, desperate day' my father greeted him 'won't clear till eleven.'

As it was sunny enough to get a suntan in bed, Stanley was even more mystified. He looked, walked over, gently removed the old boy's glasses, wiped the cream from their lenses, replaced them delicately in position and stood back.

'Good Lord', said my father with a sweet smile. 'It's cleared up quicker than I thought!'

A few minutes later Stanley was in my room:

'Either that fellow's the biggest fox I know or he's gone stark staring mad!'

My room at Eton overlooked the old fives courts and every evening a large number of swifts would make use of these irregular obstacles as a test of their flying skills. I used to watch them after prayers when we were all confined to our separate rooms for the night, and this intrigued my housemaster Mr C. M. Wells when he dropped by on his passage round. He was a great classical scholar and insatiably curious about all aspects of life. I would talk to him about birds and he would cap whatever fact I produced by citing learned parallels from Aristophanes or some other of the ancients. In my second year I had to spend the summer term at Hirsel with suppressed measles. Rest and inactivity were the cure and much of my time was spent sitting in a deck-chair in the lea of the East wing of the house, watching a screaming pack of swifts from Coldstream trying to gain possession of a single natural nesting site under the guttering. It seemed to me then that there had to be a way of catering for the needs of the disappointed birds, which so clearly preferred to nest on the house than in the town, but I did not discover it till my successful development of a swift-box over thirty years later. However my preference for swifts as the most mysterious and rewarding of birds was fixed, and it still is.

By the time I got to Oxford, George was beginning to show signs of being the keenest naturalist in the family. I taught him the rudiments of observation, that patience and stillness are essential and that if you sit quietly even the shyest bird will resume its business. Soon he was taking photographs and operating a canvas hide, a process which had to be speeded up once his time was limited to school holidays. The easiest way of doing this was to take advantage of the inability of birds to count. Someone would accompany George to his hide, he would slip inside and his companion would return the way he had come, talking merrily as he went to disguise George's disappearance. Often Collingwood accompanied him on these expeditions, especially the early morning ones when I was still soundly asleep, and that long-suffering man consequently earned the reputation for being slightly touched in the head, having been seen talking and gesticulating to himself as he hurried back alone through the park to prepare the house for the day ahead.

Subsequently my father bought George a very old-fashioned tripod camera. It took a lot of setting up but the lenses were excellent. All George's extant photographs were taken with this camera which he used at Eton and elsewhere, though 80% of his work was done at Hirsel. Had he survived the War, I am sure he would have made bird and animal photography his career. As it was he joined up under age, became a pilot in the R.A.F. and disappeared on a training flight over the Pacific in 1942. Even bearing in mind that his photographs in this book were taken with very cumbersome equipment when he was a schoolboy, they still seem the equal of the best professional work of their time

My days at Oxford over I had to get a job, so I went to London and became an estate agent. I used to play a lot of bridge and one evening a school friend of mine, Seymour de Lotbinière, in those days Director of Outside Broadcasts for the B.B.C., asked if we could interrupt our game at seven o'clock because he wanted to listen to a live broadcast he had initiated on birds. We turned on the wireless and as far as I was concerned heard absolutely nothing for half-an-hour. After it was over Seymour asked our opinion.

'If anyone had switched that on hoping to hear birds they wouldn't have learned a thing,' I said. He was rather put out.

'Do you think you could do better?'

'I couldn't do worse!' I replied.

So he stamped off in a fury. Two weeks later I was rung up by Brian Johnston with the suggestion that we should do some outside broadcasts of birdsong together. Seymour had called my bluff. I accepted at once, and I must say that, in retrospect and given the primitive recording conditions of the time, we succeeded in producing some wonderful series.

In my years as an outside broadcaster recording techniques did not change. Usually a control hut was erected and four or five cables with microphones attached were run out and positioned to pick up the voices of the birds desired. The commentator was free to control proceedings from the hut or roam the area with a two-way microphone at the end of another cable, directing the engineer as to which microphones to switch to as well as delivering his commentary. Another cable connected the hut to a transmitting van which relayed the broadcast to the B.B.C. Control Centre. Sometimes everything was directed from the transmitter van, sometimes we transmitted by attaching the master cable to a land line and always, whether live or not, the recording was simultaneously cut on soft wax for preservation as a record.

Through the mid-thirties I recorded a large number of programmes – I remember one particulary arduous all night effort on nightingales in celebration of the 1935 Jubilee – but my most regular spot with Brian was a half-hour on sunday evenings just before Evensong. Meanwhile I continued my work as an estate agent in London. I had arranged things so that I could easily slip away.

Working with Brian was enormous fun, but as he was the most indefatigable practical joker I had to keep my wits about me. One of our first disputes was over recording sites. Kent and Sussex are the best English counties for songbirds and I had a wonderful selection of woods lined up at Arundel, Hever and elsewhere, but he refused to record anywhere other than at a place called Leigh – in a wood bordered by a railway line and a very busy main road. The noise was deafening and although there were birds none of them was very remarkable. I could not understand it, and no doubt the listeners were equally bemused. They must have thought it was some sort of programme about transport.

'Wonderful place,' was all that Brian would say, 'must go and have a drink with the Colonel.'

The Colonel was a very fierce Indian army type who lived

nearby. But of course it was not the Colonel who was the object of Brian's interest but the Colonel's daughter who, I am glad to say, eventually became the delightful Mrs Johnston. Once this had been fixed we were able to get back to the birds – with great success.

These happy days came to an end with the onset of the War. Having been refused entry to the Navy on medical grounds I joined the War Office, but to my relief found myself in uniform by 1940 as an A.D.C. and by the time I was a major at Scottish Command in 1941 my recording activities had begun again. My Army Commander, General Thorne, suggested I do outside broadcasts on birds on the B.B.C. World Service for our troops overseas. The sites had to be kept secret for some security reason, but nevertheless I was astonished to receive numerous letters accurately identifying many of our locations, not least Hirsel. The popularity of these programmes undoubtedly led to my becoming established as the official 'Birdman' for the Scottish B.B.C. after the War, a position I held on a variety of programmes till the regional units were disbanded in 1958 in preference for a centralised department at Bristol.

Probably the most successful of these broadcasts was 'Nature Scrapbook', which ran fortnightly on 'Children's Hour' for over six years. Three specialists – Zooman for animals, Hutman for practicalities, and Birdman – answered listeners' letters. Friends and other well-wishers used to write unrepeatable questions in childish scripts which was always hazardous because the programme went out live, and matters were made no better by Tom Gillespie, the Zooman, having as pronounced a slur as Winston Churchill. His n's, unfortunately, were particularly obscure. Once a child wrote in asking if her mother was right in forbidding her to swim in the Firth of Forth because of the danger of being stung by the tentacles of the jellyfish.

'Tell your mother she's being too cautious,' drawled Tom. 'Jellyfish in the Firth of Forth seldom have teshticles more than four inches long. Good Lord, she should count herself lucky she's not in the Arctic. I've seen some teshticles up there forty foot long at least!'

As usual on such occasions my stifled laughter forced me to leave the studio. In these years I got to know many of the personalities whose names will appear from time to time in this book: Ludwig Koch, Peter Scott, George Waterston (the man who turned Fair Isle into one of the World's most valuable ornithological stations and who was boss of the Scottish ornithologists for most of this post-war period), Percy Edwards, the legendary bird mimic, and many more.

My retirement from the Army in 1957 heralded a new era in my understanding of birds, because I travelled much more. I made a three-month journey through Central Africa in 1959 with the late Colonel Niall Rankin, the naturalist and explorer, and shortly afterwards received some wonderful opportunities of travelling round the Scottish Islands, the Baltic and Mediterranean as a lecturer on British India cruise ships. I had already lectured for the National Trust on some of their northern cruises and had a good knowledge of Scandinavia so that my Mediterranean education was an essential complement. Meanwhile at home I continued to freelance as a broadcaster both on radio and Scottish television, but my journeys were not at an end. In 1966 I remarried, and my wife's family being South African we have since made almost annual visits to that country, which for a British birdman is chiefly significant as the winter refuge for so many of our summer migrants. There too I have been lucky enough to benefit from the friendship of Colonel Jack Vincent of World Wildlife and Natal Parks Board fame, the greatest ornithologist I have met. His dismay at the terrible decline in the numbers of European nesting birds in South Africa has heightened my awareness of the desperate measures which will have to be taken if the majority of European birds, migratory and otherwise, are to survive into the next century.

At Hirsel we are still fortunate in providing a home for northern and southern migrants alike. The swifts, which I succeeded in attracting to the house in the 'fifties as I had dreamed of as a schoolboy years before, still occupy every one of the nesting-boxes provided. The dawn chorus in Dundock Wood beyond the Lake is still an almost unrecordable babel of voices. On the surface, but only on the surface, little has changed.

As a boy I was early presented with the two volumes of Muirhead's *Birds of Berwickshire* written in 1886. They have been my most constant reference ever since. I hope this book will take its place beside his, contributing some insights on a further hundred years of the life of the birds in this corner of the world. He saw the disappearance of the sea eagle and an increase in the numbers of the gamebirds. I have seen the appearance of some new species – collared dove, green woodpecker and others – but overall I have witnessed decline, especially among the songsters. I have also seen an enormous advance in our scientific knowledge of birds and a comparable growth of public interest. Ornithologically we no longer understand a bird as being of 'Berwickshire' or any other such locality, and sanctuaries like the Hirsel are now part of a global heritage. Coachloads of birdlovers arrive annually from Holland and Germany, even from the U.S.A., to see what we can show them. If my book is less parochial than Muirhead's, that is merely a reflection of this extraordinary change; as an anecdotal record of one man's good fortune in being a birdman, its spirit is the same.

## 2. | Seabirds and the lake

The most threatened species of all birds are the oceanbound seabirds. Their position becomes daily more perilous as the world's pollution is discharged into the waters of their sole environment. The British have been no better than other nations in this respect. We do not like to remember such things now, but after the last War our unused poisonous gases were brought in sealed trains to Port Ryan in Ayrshire and then taken under naval escort and sunk off the Atlantic Shelf, some in sealed containers, others only in wooden cases. There is no question that, because of this fool-hardy packaging, many of these gases have long since escaped. Now with ocean oil fields increasing the outlook seems even more sinister. Ironically the first party to set foot on and annexe the uninhabitable chunk of sheer rock called Rockall included that expert on seabirds James Fisher. Today Rockall may prove the most treasured of British possessions, granting us the ownership of a potentially enormous oil field in the north-eastern Atlantic.

## Seabirds and the lake

At Hirsel we are within thirty miles of both the famous gannetry on the Bass Rock at the entrance to the Firth of Forth and the teeming colonies of terns, gulls, cormorants and eiders on the Farne Islands off the Northumberland coast to the South, and from an early age I became equally familiar with both. But it was not until Niall Rankin asked me to accompany him and his wife on an expedition to the Treshnish Islands in 1930, that I made my first and last extended encampment on a seabird colony.

The Treshnish group lies a few miles off Mull, near enough for the bullocks to be towed across the intervening sea on the ends of ropes and released on the islands to graze themselves fat for the autumn sales at Oban; but otherwise largely unvisited. We had to heave the rocks aside to form a harbour and assemble a prefabricated hut among the stone foundations of the old settlement, abandoned for over a century, for shelter. Amazingly the house mice were still there. That first evening they emerged from the ruins to savour our supplies. Our chief interest was in a mouselike bird, the storm petrel. There was a large colony of them immediately below our hut, nesting under the stones along the shore. By day you would not have known there was a petrel there, but at dusk they crept out to feed on the plankton in the sea, continually returning to their mates and nests. As you walked along you could hear this constant mouselike chitter coming from the ground at your feet. At that time of year they are completely nocturnal. We successfully treated one with a bruised wing. It lay in a box, feeding quite contentedly at intervals on sardine oil while the bone mended, and flew again after two weeks. At sea you are much more likely to see them riding the waves. Niall filmed and I scouted, but none of the other birds were half as intriguing. We left after two weeks. Twenty years later I flew over the islands during a military exercise and there on Lunga our hut was still standing and I could just make out the little beach we had cleared for the boat.

Since then of course I have visited many islands but perhaps none of greater ornithological significance than Fair Isle, which lies between Orkney and Shetland, almost equidistant from Scotland and Norway. Fair Isle's position is crucial to the survival of countless birds both on passage and lost. It is a particularly significant landfall for American birds that have been carried on what that Fair Isle specialist, Kenneth Williamson, first described as 'Atlantic drift': a prevailing westerly airstream which makes it far more common for American birds to arrive in Europe than vice versa. Once when I was visiting the island there was great excitement because of the arrival of an American song sparrow. A rich American lady got very carried away and said she would have twenty more of the birds flown in immediately so that a colony could be started. There was much action on the ship's wireless but nothing came of it; we cruised on and, apparently, after a week the song sparrow left too. It was a very nondescript bird which would almost certainly have gone undetected anywhere but on a ringing station, and it clearly illustrated the point that rarities occur where there is the greatest concentration of bird-watchers.

The preservation of Fair Isle as a bird sanctuary and research station is entirely due to the vision of two Scotsmen, George Waterston and Ian Pitman. Before the War it was already a place of pilgrimage for dedicated ornithologists but nobody had ever thought of taking it in hand. It is not a very prepossessing island in appearance being flat and totally exposed, but George in particular had different ideas. In the War he found himself locked up in Germany as a prisoner with Ian, another excellent naturalist, and between them they decided that the one thing they would do when peace came was buy Fair Isle. And they did. At least Ian, as a lawyer, negotiated and George took possession. Subsequently he handed it over to the Scottish Ornithologists and the National Trust, thus ensuring its safety, one hopes, forever.

I made many cruises to the various islands off Scotland and few of them were without incidents as memorable in their way as the sighting of the song sparrow. Most of these cruises took place on British India ships of 20,000 tons. They were superb vessels but that is a heavy tonnage for those hazardous waters, especially when they have to be steered close enough to the various seabird colonies to satisfy the demands of over 1000 bird enthusiasts armed with cameras. One day the Captain agreed to try and pass through the narrow channel between Boreray and the equally menacing stacks of the St Kilda formation, sheer rocks rising well over a thousand feet above the ship and so close on either side that the tens of thousands of gannets were peering into our eyes. The Captain had rashly suggested that some of us 'experts' should join him on the bridge and comment over the tannoy on any aspect of interest, geological, ornithological or otherwise. Suddenly the voice of Chris Mylne, the eminent bird photographer, echoed through the ship.

'If you go quickly to the port side you will see a rare bird: the sooty shearwater!'

Every passenger (some of them fairly robust) rushed to port as if to abandon ship. In that narrow channel going at a slow speed this sudden movement of weight made us lurch dangerously. Chris came and apologised to the Captain later,

'I'm sorry sir,' he said. 'I gather I endangered the ship by calling everyone to port. The thing is I really meant starboard. I never get it right!'

'What the hell is a shitty sourwater in any case?' asked the Captain.

One of the many things I learned from these cruises was the range of people's eating habits, even so close to home as Norway or the outer isles. At Bergen, for instance, I was astonished to find stalls in the fish market selling guillemots and razorbills, and I was even more surprised to find how good they were. Indeed in Norway they have the same status as a food as grouse do in Britain. But I could not stomach the speciality of the Faeroes: wind dried raw sheep, smelling like a drain. This was once the centrepiece of a civic reception in honour of our cruise. I was very grateful to be allowed to have half a puffin while they courageously stomached the mutton. In medieval times the crafty old monks of the great monastic centres on Iona and the neighbouring islands got fed up with penitential meals of fish and started eating the juicy wild geese instead. Naturally this had to be kept secret from the authorities so they pretended the lumps of meat were barnacles picked from the rocks and debris on the shore. And that was how the barnacle goose earned its name.

Another aspect of cruises was the way in which damaged or exhausted birds would land on deck at sea. I recently published a guide for the treatment of these birds in 'The Marine Observer', part of which I include here:

'SEA BIRDS

*Food.* Some birds will eat anchovies but, generally, small birds will eat whole or chopped sardines with oil from the tin and large birds will take raw pieces of fish and thin strips of liver or beef.
*Drink.* Salt water.
*Casualties.* For broken legs or wings use a thin splint of wood firmly fixed with elastoplast.

PASSERINES (small perching birds)

*Food.* One could carry a packet of budgie or canary seed and a packet of grit which is essential. If there is no seed, then use crumbled cornflakes, grapenuts or biscuits.
*Drink.* Fresh water and a bath (a soup plate with a few stones in it to prevent the bird slipping).
*Casualties.* Usually a match and elastoplast is adequate for broken wings or legs.

BIRDS OF PREY (falcons and hawks)

*Food.* Thin strips of raw liver or beef.
*Drink.* Nothing.
These birds eat a lot and they like a dark place to sleep. They are also the easiest types to keep alive and tame.

INSECT FEEDERS (warblers, i.e. small or very small migratory land birds)

*Food.* They are almost impossible to keep alive unless one has packets of goldfish food or ants' eggs. Grit is also necessary.
*Drink.* The remarks about small perching birds apply.

Mediterranean cruises were no less enthralling than those of the Atlantic. One of the great bonuses of being a birdwatcher is that you have an interest which you can practise anywhere; you learn new species and often of course recognise birds familiar to you in Britain many miles from home. Sitting in the magnificence of Delphi I soon noticed how many nuthatches there were among the ruins, it is a wonderful place for them.

Seabirds will often come inland of their own volition quite apart from accidental visits after storms. Yetholm Loch, thirty miles inland from Hirsel, will usually have a pair of long-tailed duck through the winter, while similar stretches of water in the vicinity will not; and the divers show a no less calculated preference for one water rather than another. Shelter is all important to these birds, and for this reason lakes are often more popular with them than rivers.

The Lake at Hirsel has always been a likely haven for seabirds – the divers most of all – and of course for some of the marsh birds as well. Its creation over a century ago is in many ways the key to Hirsel's peculiar attraction to such a wide variety of species. In medieval times the Merse to either side of the Tweed used to be an unrelieved series of bogs teeming with cranes, spoonbills, egrets and bitterns. One of these bogs lay to the west of the house at Hirsel and gave off such a stench that at about the time that Muirhead was writing his book my grandfather decided he had had enough. At great expense he got rid of it. I still have chunks of bog oak like ebony which were dug out during this operation and testify to the swamp's early post-glacial origins. A twenty-seven-acre lake was eventually created and beyond it, where the diggings had been dumped over what was left of the foetid ground, a shrubbery was planted of rhododendrons and sweet smelling azaleas. Today Dundock Wood is one of the horticultural glories of Scotland but unwittingly my grandfather had also created a superb natural sanctuary for water and woodland birds.

The Lake used to support a more varied population. The bitterns have gone and the two or three pairs of great-crested grebes have dwindled to two barren birds. I was convinced that pike were responsible for the decline of the grebes – as they were for the destruction of the young of so many other birds that nested there – so we tried to clean them out. The first day three of us got forty-seven at an average weight of 15lbs. It was more or less impossible not to get one every time you threw a line out. Fishing helped lower the number, but it was an inflow of sheep dip that eventually exterminated the pike. Now there are none. But the odd thing is that since their disappearance, although great-crested grebes still visit the Lake in spring, they do not nest.

And the little grebe or dabchick, which used to be very common, has declined to a single breeding pair.

The decline of the heron and the bittern is more drastic and widespread. As a child I was most impressed by the sight of two night herons which sat in a glass case in some building in Cold-stream devoted to the display of local oddities, with a notice reading:

SHOT BY THE EARL OF HOME

IN MAY 1820

ON THEIR NEST

Not surprisingly night herons have never been recorded breeding at Hirsel again, but now even ordinary herons are scarce and have only one nesting site left in the county. They have disappeared because so many of the mature hard wood trees have been cut. Both rooks and herons favour them for nesting and the shortage often throws the birds together to the dis-advantage of the heron, which can only abide sharing a colony with the noisy rooks for a limited time. Felling is not the only cause of tree loss. In 1976 the largest heronry in Britain was in jeopardy because of Dutch elm disease.

The heron has done its best to adapt. Like rooks they will build in conifers, and even on the ground when there are no trees at all, but lack of nesting sites is not their only problem. Pollution and pesticides have deprived them of a large part of their food supply. When anglers are not catching fish they always assume someone else is, and herons have too often been killed on this account. I have seldom seen the birds eating anything but the far more fish-destructive eel, and a large part of their diet consists of frogs, insects, mice and even water-rats. They are also entirely depend-ent on the length of their legs in preying for food and therefore can only catch tiddlers, at best, in the shallows. Travelling north from London on the train in the mild winter of 1976 I saw three of them lying dead by ditches in the course of the journey to Berwick.

Bitterns were another once common bird of the Merse as the

1. At my present home, Old Greenlaw. (*Camera Press*).

2. *Left*. Self, Edward,
Rachel, Bridget, Georgie
Alec, William – The
Hirsel, 1924.  *Below*. Self
Alec and my father at
Douglas, 1928.

3. George, self and Juno – The Hirsel, 1930.

4. Pre-War photographs by my brother George, lost on a flying mission over the Pacific in 1942.    *Above*. The Lake on an autumn evening.    *Below*. The valley of the Leet from the house.

5. *Above*. Rough weather can break the moorings of the coot's nest and send it floating off with the mother still aboard, as here on the Lake at Hirsel. *Left*. Herons are very shy but George found this one when it was suffering from acute indigestion having just swallowed an enormous eel. (*George Douglas-Home*).

6. *Above*. Roe-deer at Douglas in Lanarkshire, my family's summer home. *Below*. Woodcock with chicks. (*George Douglas-Home*).

7. Master of the predatory fliers, the peregrine falcon. (*Camera Press*).

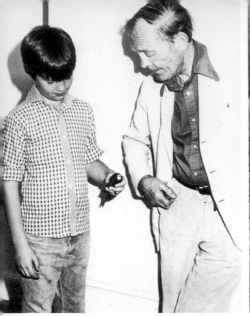

8. *Above left*. With my youngest son Peregrine at the ringing of the Hirsel swifts, 1976. This delicate operation is performed by a professional after dark at the end of the second week in July, when the adult birds have returned to the boxes to roost and the young have not yet flown. (*Tweeddale Press Group Ltd.*).   *Above right*. The original nest-boxes I designed, first occupied on this wall at Hirsel in 1953. (*Felicity Douglas-Home*).   *Below*. An early ringing session: Alec Cowieson (naturalist), Billy Murray (ringer), self, Mrs Strutt, my daughter Fiona, my mother and my sister Bridget.
(*R. Clapperton*).

many places which still incorporate its Border name of 'billy' testify, but drainage has deprived them of their habitat and they no longer breed outside a few protected fens in East Anglia. Like herons they fish by standing motionless in shallow water, their prey drifting in towards their legs and thus within range of the spearing beak. It has been said that all the birds that stand in water in this way have legs which attract fish and insects by discharging minute electrical impulses. Legs seem certainly to have an uncanny fascination for the tench, roach and, most of all, eels on which bitterns largely depend. Eels are slimy creatures and impossible to kill – they live even after you cut their heads off – and bitterns often get in a terrible tangle as they vainly try to flog the life out of them against the nearest hard surface. Usually they give this up and swallow the thing whole, their throats throbbing with the fish's exertions as it passes down. Their plumage would be impossibly clogged with slime following this performance were it not for two cleaning sacs, one placed under the wing, the other at the root of the tail. After a dirty meal they will dip their beaks into each of these in turn, first 'soaping' the feathers clean and then powdering them off to dry the slime.

The little bittern is tiny in comparison – hardly bigger than a waterhen – and beautifully plumaged in purple, green and white. It is a summer migrant to continental Europe from Africa, occasionally being blown off course on to our eastern coasts. Three years ago a perfect specimen, which is now in the Hancock Museum in Newcastle, killed itself flying into wires near the Northumberland village of Etal. Little bitterns seem to have been moving north in greater numbers recently. If a lot of birds start moving north it may mean we are in for another Ice Age, at least so I was told by a scientific friend of mine.

'In your estimation how long will that be?' I asked.

'Bit close. Too close for me on present evidence.'

'Yes, but how close? Do you think I should get some huskies?'

'20,000 years,' he said lugubriously, shaking his head. 'Not more. Not more.'

# 3. | Geese and swans

Where I live I am very lucky to be near one of the few sanctuaries of the pinkfoot goose. At Hirsel, eight miles south, I have only seen pinkfeet once in my life – being shy birds they dislike its small fields and sheltering woods – but on the edge of the Lammermuirs they have the advantage of open fields and an isolated roost out on the heather at the loch of Hule Moss. Even so I have been host to them only three times; at forty acres none of the fields on this farm are big enough to allay their fears.

The Hule Moss colony sometimes numbers as many as 5000 birds but it is not static. It represents one rendezvous of a significant proportion of the total number of birds as they pass south through Britain on their winter migration. A journey which takes them from Iceland to Montrose and, via Loch Leven and one or two of the Lammermuir mosses, to the Solway and East Anglia. These days their Greenlaw halt is briefer largely because of the food shortage caused by the rapid ploughing-in of stubbles, and for many weeks there may be no birds at all till they start to reappear in the spring on their homeward passage.

Modern farming is against them. In the past, the slower round of manual labour and an orderly rotation of crops left far richer and more varied pickings, and the birds were less harried. When I was doing work for the B.B.C. we did some research on the destruction of geese and whooper swans to crops and found no evidence to support this prejudice against them, except that they are capable of grazing a lot of grass. I discovered two old boys both over eighty, who farmed in separate parts of East Lothian. They both testified that they, and their fathers before them, believed that without geese on their fields in winter there would be a poor harvest. They prayed for geese to come. This reminded me of the practice of putting a flock of sheep on a field of winter wheat or winter-sown barley if it was getting too proud. Subsequently George Waterston and I demonstrated to an irate Tweedside farmer that a patch of winter wheat left to the mercy of a hundred whooper swans would yield twice as heavy a crop as any other part of his field. But it takes more than evidence to dispel prejudice and he tried to shoot them regardless.

In 1976 I was surprised by a visit from a senior R.A.F. officer. He said there was a major N.A.T.O. air strike exercise in the offing and he wanted to know about the movements of the geese. I told him that if they were in residence they fed once in the morning and once in the afternoon except when there was a full moon, when they went out at night. He seemed satisfied and the exercise went ahead without any disasters occurring. The Merse is a fighter training area, many of the planes rocketing across the established flight paths of the pinkfeet in and out of the Hule Moss at levels lower than the birds are capable of flying. This too has caused the geese to move on quicker than they did in pre-technological days. But for their sense I have no doubt that the inevitable crash would have happened long ago.

Few bird calls are as thrilling as the mingled cries of pinkfeet

*Pinkfooted geese*

and we went to endless trouble recording them. The most memorable occasion was one night at Fala Moss in East Lothian. Fala is a similar deposit of ice-age water to Hule Moss but much more isolated and surrounded by bogs and peat-hags: treacherous, even dangerous, ground to go into after dark. It was however a great meeting-place for pinkfeet and I knew that if we could get a cable across we would have an unforgettable recording. We ran a line out in daylight and with a great deal of difficulty finally succeeded in stretching it as far as was required. Then in good time I went into hiding in the hags and tuned into the control car on a track half a mile behind me. Reception was good so, elated, we settled down to wait. Nothing happened for an hour and then it began to freeze and darkness came on. Luckily I had a flask of whisky. Another hour passed and my clothes began to stiffen with frost. Suddenly I remembered to check the moon! It was full. Eventually one of the boys back in the car came on the line:

'We're packing it in,' he said.

'You can't do that!' I replied. 'You're not packing anything in. If you think you're cold you should come out here! The geese will be in in half-an-hour I promise,' I finished, silently cursing myself for forgetting the moon and wishing I had another flask.

'OK. We'll give you half-an-hour. Remember we've got to haul in half-a-mile of cable. Those peat-hags will be bloody lethal in the dark.'

But I was reprieved. Ten minutes later about 4000 birds came over me, at head height and in full cry. They all settled on the water and started preening and settling down for the night, buzzing like a swarm of bees. I plucked up courage and whispered into the mike:

'I hope you got all that coming in. Wasn't it terrific! Listen carefully. I'm going to do an experiment. I'm going out from this peat-hag and within five minutes from now I'm going to put them up. Is that clear? OK. Check watches.'

Accordingly I got out and squirmed over to the very edge of the water. The birds were still sawing away. The moon had broken through. I waited. Then I stood up. There was a stunned silence – there always is with geese if you surprise them, utter silence in that moment – and then the roar of their wings and a burst of sound. The noise was so terrific I instinctively shielded myself, but soon they had broken away over the moor, their agitated cries fading into the night. It took us two hours to retrieve the cable and of course the B.B.C. had omitted to bring Emergency Rations.

I could hardly wait to hear the results. Next day we met first thing at the studio for the playback: the engineers had delayed checking whether the first record had had any time left on it, and finding it had not they had been caught between discs when the birds got up. The vital sequence had been lost by a few seconds. Nevertheless enough remained to make it an unrivalled recording of the pinkfoot, worth every minute of the problems we had had in attaining it.

For all its wariness, its exceptional sight, its habit of posting sentries when it is feeding, and flying in scouts to reconnoitre the ground in advance of main parties, pinkfeet can be bemused by certain weathers, particularly fog. One evening the late Colonel Henry Trotter, Master of the Berwickshire Foxhounds, telephoned me in a great state to say that he had 'one of my pinkfeet'

(he blamed me personally for the misbehaviour of any bird in the neighbourhood) in his stable-yard, his best hunters had run amock in their stalls, the bird refused to fly off and he and his grooms could not catch it. His restraint in the circumstances was admirable. I went over to lend a hand, and the poor goose eventually took off into the night. On another occasion in similar weather the Hule Moss birds noisily circled my local village of Greenlaw all night, mistaking the gleaming reflections from the streetlights for the water on the nearby loch. Such a glint must have enticed the unhappy bird to land in Henry's yard. Surprisingly for such nervous birds pinkfeet are readily tamed.

After the War Peter Scott came to the Borders to net pinkfeet for research purposes. It worked quite well but eventually he carried out all the ringing in Iceland during the summer moult, which proved to be more or less 100 per cent successful. So Berwickshire has shared in the preservation of this marvellous bird, whose fate even now rests on the goodwill of the Icelanders who have postponed the construction of a reservoir on its breeding grounds, and the continued efforts of its greatest champion, now quite rightly Sir, Peter Scott.

Until twenty years ago you would be lucky to see any type of goose in the Tweed valley, but today greylag are common. Greylag used to be principally East Coast birds and their migration into northeast England and so to the banks of the river is inexplicable, but it is unlikely that they will spread farther north into pinkfoot country: the two species, though similar in many ways, only share the same roost in any number on Loch Leven, and even there strict segregation is observed. Greylag are the tamest of all geese in the wild and are the ancestor of the farmyard bird. A friend of mine winged one once out shooting and, to save time, instead of wringing its neck he tucked it between his legs while he shot at two more. Having missed he heard an odd sound and looking down discovered the wounded bird happily cropping the grass from between his feet. Another goose which is slowly increasing in the area much to the concern of some birdlovers who think it will start kicking out the pinkfeet, is the imported Canada. They need not worry. Canadas are the most unaggressive of birds. In 1975 two pairs bred at Hirsel for the first time. They nested in a cornfield by the Lake and when the goslings emerged children could stroke them without the parent birds showing the least dismay, other than a warning hiss which was wisely ignored.

Shooting by farmers and wildfowlers probably does far less damage to geese than might be thought. They are mostly shy birds and well padded with feathers so that big bags of them are rare. The illegality of their sale has also helped. The professional gunmen have gone and most of today's weekend wildfowlers have no conception of how near a goose has to be if it is to be brought down by the charge of an ordinary shotgun. I had a friend in Cheshire who killed a white-front whose legs were so riddled with shot that he sent it off to the Natural History Museum to be analysed. It was found to have twenty-two pellets in its body in various places including the legs, ranging in size from BB to No. 7 shot, but was nonetheless in perfect physical condition.

Of all the ways of shooting geese punt-gunning was the most lethal. The barrels were like six-inch naval guns down which, at the top end, you stuffed the 'shot' – literally anything that might make an impact; nails, screws, nuts and bolts, god knows what – loaded it at the bottom with a huge and usually home-made cartridge, pulled a piece of string and hoped for the best. As likely as not salt would have corroded something, the breech would burst and the whole lot would come back in your face. Ian Pitman, of Fair Isle fame, had this happen to him near North Berwick and returned to Edinburgh carrying one of his eyes in his hand. There was nothing to be done so he had to have a glass replacement, but he soon found that he needed three: one for when he was feeling bright eyed, one for average, and one really ghoulish one for when he had a hangover. He used to have them laid out on a velvet tray.

'Now darling,' he would say to his wife in the morning, 'which one do you think I should wear today?'

'Well you've got the most frightful hangover as usual. I should wear the purple one.'

The best excuse for shooting is to eat what you shoot, and geese can make a very good meal indeed if prepared correctly. There are many ways of doing this but I think the bird is most appetising if you slit the gizzard – geese do not have crops – and stuff it full of small onions. Then take the corpse out to the garden, dig a hole and bury it in with its tail to the north – not forgetting to mark the spot (a very important point as I have found to my cost!) – leave it for two weeks and dig it up. Most of the feathers will have gone without the trouble of skinning or plucking, and the meat will be savoury and tender. The late Lord Rosebery had an even more refined method. He had a 'goose-room' in which the birds were hung on hooks, and every day a specially appointed 'gooseman' would visit the birds and drip two drops of olive oil down each of their throats. There was a small pan under each bird and the gooseman had strict orders to continue his daily dripping until the pan was full. Lady Rosebery used to warn me: 'Never go near the goose-room. The smell is intense.' Only the gooseman could officially go there, and if Lord Rosebery had a bad bird he had hell to pay.

'You must have got fed up with your job and put three drops instead of two, because this goose is no bloody good!'

'No milord, I promise you. Always two drops a day.'

'Well this bird is bloody awful! Chuck it to the dogs!'

In the last War when the Home Fleet was anchored at various points all the way from the Moray Firth north to Scapa Flow in the Orkneys, the area was sealed off for security reasons. To enter it you had to have a pass and be cleared at Inverness. However it soon became clear to those of us in Intelligence that information was being leaked to a serious and very damaging degree. The list of suspects, the passholders who went in and out of the area most suspiciously, was reduced to six, one of them a famous London dentist. He was a mad keen wildfowler, who had been making shooting trips to the region for at least ten years. Colonel Tom Spens of G.I. Intelligence, an immaculate Cameronian (he had me arrested once) was in charge of the investigation and he asked my opinion. 'The dentist is the most obvious risk,' he said, 'but I can't fault him.'

'What does he do with the birds?' I asked.

'Takes them back to London of course.'

'How?'

'Depends how long he's up for. Sends some ahead, brings down the rest.'

'I should check the birds,' I said, and left it for him to decide. Next time the dentist appeared, the first hamper of game he sent back to London was secretly apprehended and checked. There were six pinkfeet, four mallard and various other ducks, all of them with their gizzards slit and resown to hide the shipping codes which had been inserted. The hamper was then forwarded to London where the German agent who collected it at Kings Cross was arrested, as in due course was the dentist. We never had any more trouble.

In April 1967 five snow geese stayed for a month on the fields east of Carham on the southern bank of Tweed. They returned at the same time for the next four years, which indicated that they were definitely migrating birds although probably ones that had been reared here domestically and allowed to revert to a wild state. A blue ring seen on one of their legs further supported my theory. Most rare geese in this country will be escaped or semi-domesticated, although occasionally genuine strays do appear in the ranks of the commoner species.

Some idea of the age to which geese can live may be gauged by a snow goose discovered by Niall Rankin. Niall was filming birds in Alaska and met an old farmer. He asked how he could best locate and photograph snow geese to which the old man replied: 'No bother. Come here in the morning and see Jeannie. She's sitting on fourteen eggs in my haystack.' Next day Niall returned. The old man told him that he had found the bird as a gosling with a broken leg forty-four years before. He had mended the leg by riveting it with a piece of iron and by this mark he knew that she had returned to raise a brood on the farm every year since. There was Jeannie unmoved on her nest and there, when the old man lifted one of her legs, was the crude, rusty rivet. Niall was so intrigued that he got in touch with the old man the next summer. Unluckily, or perhaps through old age, Jeannie had not returned.

When people in this country say they have seen a swan – the swan you throw bread to from the tow-path or in your local park, the swan you see with cygnets in the spring – it is the mute swan. They are often unaware that there are two other swans, the whooper and the bewick, which are as wild as, though less shy than, the geese and migrate here from much the same latitudes for the winter months. Both birds are commoner on Tweedside today than at any time in my life, particularly the whooper despite its failure to adapt to the presence of electric pylons. They can often be found dead in the fields having hit the cables.

On Tweed mutes are numerous enough to be a pest, although they do do some good by dislodging weed from the bottom of the river, but on the whole they are troublesome: they disrupt fishing, kill the young of other birds in their territories and, in the breeding season they even kill each other in ferocious duels between rival males. Throughout the breeding season swans should be treated with respect as they are quite capable of maiming children in defense of their nests. The most humane way of controlling their numbers is by pricking a few eggs so that the female sits out the spring on a clutch that will hatch two or three, instead of five or eight, cygnets.

Recording such noiseless birds for the B.B.C. in an interesting way was always a problem, especially if I had children in tow to ask questions and liven up the programmes. One time at Hirsel I took out three children, including a particularly objectionable eight-year old who always tried to get the better of me, to record a female mute on its nest. The male bird was a long way down the Lake feeding, the female (who I knew very well) was serenely sitting, so we decided to proceed. I lifted her gently to show the eggs to the children, commentating all the time, and was generally employed when this little terror of a boy said in the most casual way imaginable that there was a swan approaching. As we were in the middle of the recording I naturally did my best to cover-up this interference when, too late, I sensed danger. Lifting my head I saw we were about to be attacked by the angriest swan I have ever seen in my life. I had to round off the recording quietly and convincingly but I also had to evacuate the children:

'So here comes father swan now,' I said as evenly as possible, scrambling backwards. 'Here he comes to see that all is well. . . .' With which the bird hurled itself at me and all pretence of calm had to go by the board. We fled into the reeds.

'What happened there?' they asked back at the recording car. To my horror I realised that I had arrived with only two children. My persecutor was missing.

'Well,' I said mildly, 'I thought we'd done enough. I think we covered everything. . . .'

'Major, I didn't think we retreated in very good order did we?' Interrupted a well-known voice.

'Where have you been you little twister!' I exclaimed.

'Up a tree,' he smiled. 'So I got a very good view of you all running away!'

## 4. | Tweed and ducks

The Tweed is a wonderful place for watching wildlife and never better than when one is fishing. The boatman and I seldom spoke and I found complete peace with nature and myself: the slow beat of the oars, the volume and variety of the birds going to roost or ducks flighting out to feed. Almost every evening a whistle would be heard, or one or more shapes be seen crossing the water below us: otters on their journey. We would hold against the current and watch them as they came playfully like dolphins. There was a great harmony of beauty in their movement. Our aim of catching a final fish before dark became incidental to the more lasting value of the twilight: peewits, owls, ducks, otters, and still old Tweed meandering to the sea.

One of my earliest memories is of my father coming into the hall at Springhill, the Home dower house in which I was brought up, and laying down a 42lb salmon on the carpet. A wooden replica of that mighty fish hangs at Hirsel to this day. Unlike Hirsel, secluded in its park, Springhill stands open to the Tweed and from infancy our greatest treat was to play on its banks or be taken out by one of the boatmen.

No one, not even Sir Walter Scott, has adequately described Tweed. On its ninety-five mile journey to the sea it is bent double by the hills, squeezed into torrential rapids, shallowed by ridges of shingle and, as it wanders with deceptive calm past Hirsel, released into pools of great depth and danger. On the Birgham beat below Springhill the stretch called the Weil Rock seems as harmless as the arrowed ripple at its tail which marks the presence of the Rock itself. And yet when Tom Scott, the boatman, fished out the tenant's half-hunter watch after it had fallen overboard, he had to use the full length of a forty foot rope to reach the bottom, and that was at low water in the summer. The Weil is a huge cavern carved out by the grinding rocks of the Ice Age, its placid surface disguising a stream always running at full strength.

One day Angus Cunningham-Graham, in the war the senior admiral in Scotland, telephoned me to ask if I could arrange a day's fishing for his superior, Sir Philip Vian, then admiral of the entire Home Fleet. Vian was a legend, the Nelson of his time, so naturally I was most flattered to be of use. I rang my father and a date was fixed, the worst as far I was concerned because it co-incided with one of my B.B.C. broadcasts in Dundock. However, when the morning arrived I felt obliged to be on hand to welcome such distinguished visitors and see them off to their fishing. Broadcasts took most of the day to prepare, so I was rather irritated to be kept waiting by the admirals, who eventually arrived with outriders and two huge limousines about one hour late. Vian looked sinister with his enormous drooping eyebrows and rather sullen, while Cunningham-Graham explained that they had been delayed by missing the ferry! 'You missed the ferry, jolly good show,' I said.

'Well,' explained Cunningham-Graham, 'this trip's a bit *sub rosa* so we thought we'd use the ferry instead of the admiral's barge.'

This was all very incongruous but I was late, the wind was light and blowing perfectly upstream, so the sooner they got out in the boats the better. Sir Philip still looked furious at having missed the ferry, but he was soon on his way with Lady Vian and Struthers, the second Birgham boatman, to the lower beat, while Cunningham-Graham was rowed off upstream. I then rushed back to Dundock to get a few things arranged before lunch.

I returned at 12.45 just in time to greet the Vians as they came off the water. Sir Philip's eyebrows were drooping another fifteen degrees, Struthers was his inscrutable self and Lady Vian looked distinctly unwell. Struthers was famous for his outspokeness, so I immediately assumed that he was the cause of the gloom. 'How did you get on?' I asked Lady Vian as she passed, but she appeared too ill to reply. 'Two fish,' said Vian gravely. 'I'd like to have a few words with you.' My heart sank. Apparently shortly after they had started fishing the Admiral had noticed what he took to be a turnip bobbing astern, but his mind was soon distracted by his hooking a fish. As he played it and it slowly ran back upstream he began to realise that the 'turnip' was the head of a drowned man.

'There's a dead man there,' he exclaimed.

'Aye, yon's a corpse,' said Struthers laconically. 'It's got a look of Lord Home, now I think about it.'

'Hadn't we better get it out?' asked the Admiral.

'Just you keep your eye on the fish, Admiral,' ordered Struthers. 'He'll still be there tonight in this wind.'

The Admiral was a bit shaken by this but he did as he was told and eventually they netted the fish. No sooner had Struthers knocked it on the head than he put out again.

'We aren't going on?' Asked the dumfounded Admiral.

'Aye, you get a line out as quick as you can,' said Struthers stolidly. 'There's more fish there.'

'But we can't just leave it!'

'Admiral Vian, I'm surprised at you,' said Struthers, leaning on the oars and taking out his pipe. 'Here's you whose filled the North Sea with dead Germans making a fuss about one old body in Tweed. I'll get him out the night.'

The Admiral hooked another salmon as before and steered it round the bobbing corpse while Lady Vian began to be sick in the bows and Struthers silently smoked his pipe. The netting of this second fish and lunchtime called a halt to the macabre spectacle, which was when I arrived.

I roared off to the police station in Coldstream immediately. 'Where's the Sergeant?' The Sergeant was at a cricket match. But he was not at the cricket either, he had gone off to have a shave and a haircut. He was halfway through when I burst into the barbers.

'You've got to come at once!' I said agitatedly. 'There's a body in Tweed. Admiral Vian.'

'Is it the Admiral?' Asked the sergeant, not in the least surprised.

'No, of course not,' I said, as he followed me out into the street half-bearded and half-shorn.

The body was spinning in the eddy a few feet off shore in deep water. It was quite clear that the sergeant, being in his weekend best, was not going to jump in so eventually I had to. When the corpse was finally beached the sergeant said he required the man's proof of identity. 'Identity? Now!' 'Aye, we'll have to search his pockets.' A gruesome search of the soaking clothes produced no more evidence than a soggy packet of 'Players' cigarettes, a brand I have never smoked since. An hour later we had succeeded in removing the little old man (a suicide as it was subsequently established) from the scene by winching him to a tractor. The bank was too steep to afford any other way.

After a rather distracted and ill-prepared broadcast I returned to Hirsel for a drink with my guests before they left for Rosyth. Sir Philip repeated the story to my father: 'Struthers said it might have been you,' he said. 'Oh was it?' said father, but as usual he was far more sensible than he ever let people think. 'The only thing that worries me,' said the Admiral, 'is that I shall have to appear as a witness at the inquest.'

'Which bank was he landed on?' Asked my father.

'The North,' I said.

'You won't have to worry about an inquest Sir Philip,' he said. 'We don't have a coroner in Scotland.'

The Scots and English never risked wading Tweed except at well-known fords although they fought over it for hundreds of years. At the end of the War I was asked to advise on some military maneouvres in the area. I warned them to be particularly careful of the river and not to wade it on any account. Two men were drowned in the dark.

Tweed is wonderful for birds, for rarities like the black-winged stilt and the black tern, kingfishers and sandmartins and grazing herds of whooper swans, but most of all for ducks. Its banks provide good shelter and Hirsel being near the sea, almost all the European varieties have appeared over the years. Apart from inland dabblers and divers I have seen scoters, scaups, smews regularly, long-taileds, shellducks and several more. But my eye was always caught by the drake goosanders. In winter, particularly, a little pack of half-a-dozen of them standing against the snow in their regalia of pinks, scarlets, greys, whites, blacks and bottle green, made them for me the most beautiful of all that excessively beautiful family.

Goosanders and mergansers, the diving sawbilled ducks, are fish eaters and still treated as vermin by some fishermen and water authorities. Until ten years ago the Tweed Commissioners offered a reward of 2s. 6d. for a goosander head, a practice now thankfully discontinued. A brief inspection of the gizzard of either bird will reveal that, like the heron, it predominantly eats the sort of fish that do most harm to salmon and trout: perch, roach and, above all, eels. Eels are secretive things but their consumption of salmon and trout spawn as they creep along the bottom of a river is far more damaging than the loss of the odd salmon parr to a sawbill. On Tweed we principly have goosanders, tree-hole nesters, unlike the west coast mergansers which breed in rushes and on the moors like the majority of the other ducks.

Both these birds are partially resident in Britain but for some reason that other tree nester the goldeneye was not until 1970, when a pair was induced to occupy a nest-box on Speyside. In Scandinavia they have been making them nest artificially in this way for years, goldeneye 'farming' being a long established cottage industry. The design of the boxes is based on the nest-holes of black woodpeckers, whose sites are the ones most commonly used by goldeneye in the wild, and measure approximately 42″ × 14″. The duck nest in the boxes and the farmers remove a proportion of the down and eggs three times before allowing the females to brood. In this way they gather 2lbs of down and 18 eggs per box. Some farmers own over a hundred boxes so it is easy to imagine how profitable the business can be. Often goldeneyes stay on the Lake at Hirsel well into May and having seen the drakes performing their elaborate courtships I decided to try out some of these boxes among the trees at the water's edge. Whether the goldeneye were interested or not was never revealed because the popularity of the contraptions with other species of birds did not allow the wretched duck a look in. If I succeeded in keeping the jackdaws at bay, the next visit would disclose a new lodger: stockdoves, barn and tawny owls, thrushes, even, and most unusually, a redstart. Eventually I passed the idea on to George Waterston and abandoned the project. George tried to interest the Loch Leven goldeneye, but eventually it was the Speyside boxes which provided the first breeding pair in Scotland.

Of all birds ducks are probably the best parents, extremely protective of their young and endlessly resourceful in the face of all dangers, from foxes to floods. Eiderducks are notably courageous sitters. On the Farne Islands several pairs nest among the ruins of the old chapel, undisturbed by the endless parties of tourists who trudge within a few feet of them every day. During incubation the ducks can even be lifted off their eggs. The reason for such tight sitting is undoubtedly their much greater fear of scavenging animals and birds. Gulls and crows are very vigilant, and if they see an eider sitting they will chivvy her until she moves and offers them the freedom of her nest. Shelduck are more organised. They have a unique 'kibbutz' system whereby one or two adult females will look after all the ducklings while the rest of the colony has the day off. When the breeding season is over most of our shelduck leave for a brief stay in Holland, no one quite knows why.

Teal are equally resourceful with their young. They are moorland nesters, and a brood I once discovered convinces me that in certain circumstances they, like woodcock, are capable of carrying their young. This particular bird had chosen to nest a few yards inside a young moorland plantation of scotch firs. The trees were surrounded by a new, stoutly stobbed, wire fence, and since the mesh was far too fine for even a teal duckling to squeeze through and far too tight at the bottom to be burrowed under, we wondered how on earth the female was going to extricate her brood. Of course she managed, the whole family duly appearing on a nearby loch, but not when we were there to record it, so the mystery remained. I see no way in which she could have got the birds out without holding them between her thighs and flying each one over in turn.

On another occasion I was no less bamboozled by a shoveller. We had never discovered a shoveller's nest at Hirsel, so when I happened to see a settled looking pair on a half dried up mill pond I began to keep a watch. They were undoubtedly nesting. The little pond was on the edge of a field of newly sown barley and from time to time the female would waddle into it a few yards and then vanish. Meanwhile the drake was usually away, no doubt consorting with other females down on the Lake. But when I searched there was no sign of her: a slight dip in the land which could account for her momentary but not permanent disappearance, and that was all. The earth was bare except for the fringes of barley sprouts. I could not understand it. The crop grew and I gave up looking, convincing myself of the nest's non-existence, until one day there was the old lady on the mill-pond with a brood of ducklings. That was the final straw! I carefully entered the crop where I had originally investigated and crawled over the ground until I found the nest, the most surprisingly small one I have ever seen, set perfectly in a horse's hoofmark.

Mallard are commonly ground nesters but at Hirsel they have a peculiar though sensible habit of using holes in trees. This must have originated as a defence against predators, but although Berwickshire is a fine area for foxes I cannot explain why Hirsel mallard should seek to protect themselves in this way so much more frequently than in other places. Here, for a long time was another mystery for me: how did the duck bring the ducklings down? Eventually the head gardener witnessed the performance.

One day coming into the garden at about 7 o'clock in the morning he heard a great quacking going on. The height of the wall cut off his view, so he crept to the gate and there was the duck mallard at her nest thirty feet up in the broken branch of an old oak tree, with the ducklings toppling over the edge and floating to the lawn like thistle-down. It became clear that one final duckling was unprepared to jump. The quackings became more and more frantic until the mother knocked it off the branch with her bill. Then she led the whole brood waddling off to the lake three hundred yards away.

The first days out of the nest are as difficult for mallard as for any other bird. Pike seize them from below; mute swans drown them; weasels, stoats, foxes, the scavenging birds like crows and gulls, prey on them by land. Nor are matters improved by the timing of the adult moult. The young will still not have fledged when the adults, like wild geese, become grounded and equally helpless as they wait for their flight feathers to grow during July. Any reedbed at that time of year will reveal scores of skulking duck if you put a dog through it.

Grain is the mallard's favourite food and in autumn they will invade the harvest fields in great numbers, usually at dusk to ensure a few hours of uninterrupted feeding before retiring to have a drink. If it were not for man I am sure they would as readily feed by day, but his presence over the centuries has turned them, like so many of the waterfowl, into semi-nocturnal birds. Resting on water by day and flying forays by night is now the normal routine for most of them. Mallard are as adaptable in their feeding as in everything else. They are potato, weed, bread and scrap feeders in cities, and carnivores – liking nothing better than rabbit guts, and in London even being reputed to have guzzled the odd live sparrow. In other words they are omnivorous. If guts go missing from flight ponds, however, it could be the no less omnivorous waterhen that is the culprit. One October at Hirsel I was most surprised to come across a hundred or so mallard wolfing down acorns in the depths of an oak wood. The trees were still in full leaf and the noise of their landing through the branches was like a downpour.

Their sexual appetite is no less robust. Mallard are responsible for more half-castes than any other duck species. The most recent example I have seen was a bird that looked like a mallard except it had a purple head, blue bill and the splayed feet of a diving duck. It could have been a scaup cross but we decided that a tufted was much more likely. There have been examples of such crosses with most resident ducks, the rapacious drake mallard invariably being the common factor. By March and April the females are mostly sitting on eggs and the drakes gather on lakes and reservoirs keeping a weather eye for the few remaining unattached birds. They seldom play any part in the support and upbringing of the broods, and their promiscuity appears to make any sort of paternality out of the question.

This is not entirely the mallard's fault. The females of all duck species except the shelducks are dowdy and in many cases indistinguishable from each other. The males too require camouflage when they are grounded by the moults, and for a large part of the year this renders even the sexes impossible to differentiate except at close quarters. As duck are difficult to approach in the wild and most of them migrate to the Arctic to breed and are therefore never seen here in the glory of their full breeding plumage, many people consider them to be duller birds than they deserve. No doubt such difficulties in detection make us also miss more rarities than is normally the case. A friend of mine who is very fond of his food went flighting one evening and after the bag had been counted the host invited each guest to pick up a brace of whatever he wanted. My friend was more choosey than the others and in his search for a tasty teal or wigeon, he turned up a bird which had been counted as a female goldeneye, but which he, with a reasonable knowledge of birds, was sure he had never seen before. He brought it over for me to identify the next day and it turned out to be a young drake harlequin, an Icelandic duck which has only been recorded a very few times in Britain.

All duck are long flyers, moving with the weather and often migrating considerable distances. Two teal were shot at Hirsel one winter which turned out to have been ringed as ducklings four months before 2000 miles east of Moscow – the Russians are exemplary naturalists. Most migratory birds of all species resident and otherwise will eventually return to nest at the northernmost point of their life when the breeding season returns. Mallard may migrate out of Britain but within Britain they will be moving too. A bird hatched in Fife and wintering on Hirsel Lake will fly the forty odd miles north when the next spring comes, and similarly Hirsel birds will return from their raids over the Border. In Britain the only exception to this pattern is the garganey. It migrates north, but it is a summer migrant, a few arriving from Africa to nest as the majority of our ducks are leaving.

Three years ago my nephew Jamie Douglas-Home arrived on my doorstep with a garganey he had recently shot by mistake in Lanarkshire. I confirmed his identification but asked a trusted neighbour of mine – a prominent Edinburgh businessman – to hand the bird over with an accompanying explanation from me to John Murray, the taxidermist at the Royal Scottish Museum in Edinburgh, for official notification. Two days later I received the following acknowledgement:

My dear Henry,

Thank you very much for the duck which I received in a polythene bag.

Having carried out a painstaking post-mortem examination, I remain puzzled by the whole affair. Why an ornithologist of your reputation and standing should require verification of the identity of a duck mallard (albeit in immature plumage) I cannot understand. Did I miss something? It did have a slightly enlarged liver for a bird of its age and was missing a few secondaries from the left wing, but otherwise it seemed quite normal to me.

Anyway it was delicious and my wife and I would like to thank you for what turned out to be an excellent meal.

*Yours*

JOHN

P.S. The ones with the long beaks are shovellers.

I naturally replied in some anger.

*By the same hand which delivered the duck*

Prof. John Murray, B.F.
(Expert Duck Eater)
The Royal Scottish Museum
Chamber St
Edinburgh

My dear Professor,

I'm glad you both had a good 'high' supper – I'd no idea that Museums starved their experts. But:
  (1) That bird was $\frac{1}{3}$ the size of any mallard (except 3–4 weeks old).
  (2) It had dark grey beak and legs.
  (3) Its wings were roughly:
        Forewing: Blue Grey
        Secondaries: Green (not blue mauve) as in Mallard.
  (4) It had a small beak – not a shoveller.

## Tweed and ducks

What a pity you were so hungry that you had to eat the feathers and legs.

HENRY

P.S. I wish I had told you what to do with the beak.

The answer came by return.

*Dear Henry,*

Flattered as I am by your reference to me as 'Professor', and impressed as I am by your powers of observation, nevertheless your insistence in this matter is surprising.

The bird you describe appeared to be a blue-winged teal or a garganey if indeed a duck at all. Did it have webbed feet? If not of course the mind reels. How about a great grey shrike or a black backed gull? Although the latter's feet are webbed too which adds to the confusion. Was the bird shot while swimming or flying?

I feel we must get to the bottom of this mystery.

*Yours*

JOHN

I can only thank John Murray for allowing me to expose this fraud here in the hope that it will be an example of the hazards of our profession and show the degree to which our efforts to identify rare birds can be thwarted by the practical folly of such tricksters as Jamie Douglas-Home and my neighbour Mr Alex McEwen. They of course were the 'John Murray' of the correspondence, having never intended to deliver the duck from the outset. The last letter of this regrettable correspondence will I am afraid have to remain unpublished.

Jamie Douglas-Home being the son of that incorrigible trickster my brother William, I should have been forearmed. When Alec was Foreign Secretary he returned one weekend to the peace and quiet of Hirsel for some restful fishing and the chance to compose an important speech. As he was preparing to leave for the river on Saturday morning the telephone rang. It proved to be Sir Winston Churchill long-distance from London.

'Dunglass!' roared the well-known voice – he always addressed Alec by the name he had borne as an M.P. before succeeding to my father's title. 'If you were still serving with me I should have to remove you!' And then proceeded to vehemently criticise some aspect of foreign affairs. Slowly recognition dawned:

'William? For heaven's sake!' exclaimed Alec with exasperation, and quickly terminated the conversation.

Two hours later when he was out fishing my sister-in-law Elizabeth answered a transatlantic call from the White House, and was told that the President required to speak to the Foreign Secretary as a matter of the greatest urgency and would be calling again at lunchtime. Alec was very perturbed. The call duly came through.

'Mr President?'

'Now look here Alec what's going on over there with your Foreign Office?' came the voice of JFK. William again.

Alec went fuming back to the river to cool off and recollect his thoughts before returning towards the end of the afternoon finally to complete his speech. No sooner had he begun than he was interrupted by yet another telephone call.

'Is that you Lord Home?' asked a Scottish voice. 'I'm wondering would you be interested in 3000 women?'

'William!' Roared Alec, and he finally gave vent to his verbal frustrations of the day before slamming down the receiver once and for all. He was just telling Elizabeth that he did not want to take any more calls from William or anyone else when the telephone rang again. Elizabeth answered.

'Is that Birgham 216?' a Scottish voice said timidly. 'Thank heaven's for that. I must have had the wrong number because I've just had some very rude things said to me. This is the Moderator of the Church of Scotland speaking . . . I was wondering if Lord Home would address a conference of 3000 women this summer in Edinburgh?'

## 5. | *Africa and birds of prey*

In 1959 I went on another expedition with Niall Rankin but this time it was of a much more demanding sort than our visit to the Treshnish Islands all those years before. Niall had been given an assignment to film some of the most primitive tribes of Central Africa and when he asked me to accompany him I accepted immediately. I assumed, apart from anything else, that it would be an ornithological revelation, and the brief seemed broad enough to include film of natural phenomena other than people. We set out from Tangier in an Austin Gypsy just after New Year, and three months later arrived at Entebbe from where I returned to Scotland.

The birds were not quite as dramatic as I had hoped, largely because of the terrain, but I recall some of the journey's highlights with great pleasure, particularly our meetings with the tribes.

One blistering hot day we arrived at a village to find a guard of honour lined up in readiness outside the chief's hut. It was exactly like Buckingham Palace, fixed bayonets and all, only when we got closer we realised that they were not bayonets but superbly erect members, each one delightfully encased in a beautifully worked bamboo scabbard. Apart from that the guard was completely naked. The chief was stone-cold drunk, although it was only ten in the morning, but courtesy itself, and with his men in attendance we made the rounds. This took two hours and throughout that time the guard continued to remain at attention. I could not make it out. Eventually while Niall was filming I took the interpreter aside and asked, somewhat diffidently, if it would be possible to obtain one of these scabbards. Nothing could be easier, for a token gift one would be made for me within half-an-hour. And he was right. Thirty minutes later a charming boy came running back and handed me this bamboo thimble.

'This is rather small,' I protested.

'I'm sorry sir,' said the interpreter. 'He's summed you up and he obviously thinks that's the size that will suit you!'

My memories of the birds on this trip were completely eclipsed by my experiences on later trips to Natal, which must have the best nature reserves in the world. Every sort of habitat abounds – lagoons, salt estuaries, savannahs, plains, tropical forests – and the numbers of birds and bird species, 850 in all, is overwhelming. Here were the swifts, the swallows and warblers we only see for three months of the year in this country, plus the African species of these and other birds: not one but six species of nightjar, a dozen varieties of kingfisher. But most of all it was the birds of prey that amazed me.

In Britain we rarely see any apart from the motorway kestrels and, for all the publicity surrounding the plight of the peregrine, in my experience few people are really interested in them. They are so seldom seen: songbirds and riverbirds can be fed or watched or listened to, gamebirds can be husbanded and the surplus eaten, but birds of prey keep out of sight. Their whole object is to be inconspicuous, like all hunters, but being at the very end of the food chain they collect our poisons as inexorably as does the sea. Even in South Africa drastic and very damaging changes are now taking place, but there is still food enough to support them in numbers we have not seen here since the Middle Ages. In the Drakensburg Mountains in Natal, I saw a lammergeir – largest and rarest of eagles – an extraordinary bird which feeds by dropping bones on the mountain sides from great heights and then picking the marrow from the broken shafts. And on a ten mile stretch of the road from the Cape to Natal I counted over three hundred steppe buzzards on the telegraph poles alone. This is indicative of the variety and proportion of the numbers of all birds required if South Africa is to continue supplying Europe with so many of its most attractive but ominously dwindling flow of summer migrants.

On my earlier visit to Africa I skirted Lake Chad, home of the osprey for nine months of the year. The Lake is an enormous inland sea to the south of the Sahara. All the rivers of the area run into it and then disappear, the reason being that it is a relic of the Old Sahara which used to be irrigated by rivers running to the Atlantic and then got sandbound. It is to swamp areas like Chad, where they suffer inordinantly from mosquitoes, tsetse fly and the like, that we and other European nations have sold so many of our surplus or banned poisons. In Chad, when I was there, there was no sensible direction in the use of these poisons, and in principle I do not believe much has changed: the numbers of our summer migrants continue to decline. The fostering of the ospreys on Loch Garten and elsewhere in the Highlands will be of little avail if the birds return to Africa merely to render them-selves sterile on poisons for the remaining three-quarters of each year. International agreements and controls, however high sounding, are meaningless because there is no authority with the legal right to impose them. The abuse by all countries of oceanic agreements makes that quite clear. The food requirements of birds of prey and seabirds make them the most ecologically vulnerable to such pollution.

Ospreys left this country before the First World War, driven out by rapacious naturalists because the rarer they got the more valuable they became as 'scientific' specimens, their eggs being sold for large sums to collectors. Now in the last twenty years they have trickled back. They prefer large stretches of still water but I have often seen single birds at Hirsel on their way to and from the little Loch Garten colony two hundred miles to the north. These usually hang about the quieter parts of Tweed, reports of the movements of a single bird from all parts of the river invariably giving people the overall impression that there is a flock of ospreys in the neighbourhood. One was even seen by one of our bird-watching parties flying in front of their bus with a fish gripped in its talons. When Alec returned exhausted from his duties as Foreign Secretary for a three-week vacation, he found that there was this equally rare bird roosting every night in an oak tree within thirty yards of his bedroom window. So the osprey has come back, but its destiny, although it may one day be on our conscience, is no longer in our hands. Meanwhile its successful reintroduction has led to some efforts being made on Fair Isle and Mull to do the same for that other fish eating eagle that was once a British resident, the white-tailed sea eagle. There seems no reason why these experiments should not meet with equal success, though one can never be certain: the marsh harriers are now almost extinct as a breeding species in Britain yet, as I discovered on a summer holiday in 1975, only a few hundred miles south on the Île de Rhé off the west coast of France, the marsh harrier, if not the montague's, is a common bird.

The fortunes of all the birds of prey have fluctuated alarmingly since the 1880s when Muirhead recorded the gradual disappearance of the sea eagle from Berwickshire. Fifteen odd years ago it seemed as if even the sparrowhawk was doomed. Poisons and gamekeepers had almost eradicated them, but governmental controls of agrochemicals through a number of increasingly strict schemes and the forbearance of keepers, once they acknowledged the gravity of the situation, have given them a new lease of life. The sparrowhawk has been consciously and successfully protected, its recovery, with the possible exception of the osprey, perhaps our most praiseworthy achievement in this field since the War. Kestrels, buzzards and merlins have helped themselves by adaptation.

Buzzards were almost lost when myxomatosis temporarily destroyed the rabbit. Rabbits have survived and are now building up an immunity to the disease but in the meantime the buzzard has drastically altered its diet, scavenging off all forms of carrion and channelling its hunting instincts into the capture of frogs, rodents and even beetles. This, combined with the increase of Forestry Commission planting in England and Wales, has made it comparatively common once again and over a much broader range.

Kestrels have shown the most spectacular growth in numbers because of the voles and mice with which we unwittingly provided them by creating the rough pasture banks of the motorways. Kestrels are the least shy of the hawks and falcons and long ago adapted to city life, but just how long they will maintain their present population depends on how much of the motorway banking is planted up. A considerable amount already has been, and by the mid-'eighties when the trees have out-grown the grass the kestrel will suffer a proportionate decline.

In Berwickshire one can see that merlins too are adapting. They used to be an entirely moorland bird but today I see them far more frequently among the woods and fields of the Merse. Of the other birds of prey resident in this area, and Britain generally, only the hen harrier remains in any numbers. As for the peregrine, only sixty fledged throughout the country in 1976.

The peregrine is my favourite of all the birds of prey. Its stoop

is the most breathtaking action of any bird and something that haunts you forever once you have seen it. I have witnessed it three times, and can only describe it as being like a divebomb attack from an aeroplane. One of the most remarkable features is the amount of noise created by its speed, which can be as much as 200 mph. The three attacks were all made by the same bird, a creature which appeared to have been tamed at some point because it used to roost on the ledge of a blank window on the top floor of the old castle of our summer home at Douglas, in Lanarkshire, and never seemed particularly worried by humans. The first time I saw it I was hidden by some rushes in a bog up on the hill. Walking in I had disturbed a curlew and as I watched this bird climb the sky I noticed a peregrine circling about three hundred feet above it. Caught between opposing evils the curlew flew higher and higher calling anxiously as it went. Suddenly the falcon fell from the sky, hit the curlew with a crack like a whip, and soared away leaving the corpse spinning gently to the ground

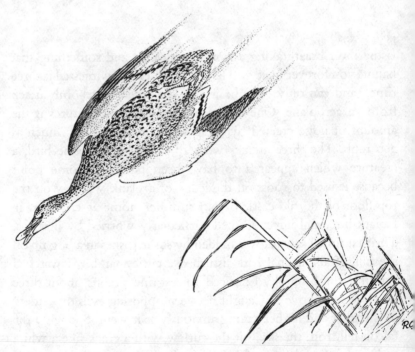

*Peregrine and Mallard*

64

on outspread wings with the severed body and head falling separately. The peregrine then settled, picked up the carcase and made off with it. The next time it showed an even greater disregard for my presence. We were driving the lake in the park. Someone fired a shot and when the duck rose in a great pack, the peregrine soared off the island. It made a point high overhead as the duck sorted themselves into their various broods and species. One particular family of mallard dangerously attracted its attention by levelling out at a greater height than the others. When the peregrine stooped, the bird it had selected closed its wings and came hurtling down, quacking with terror, head first into the water twenty yards from where I was hiding. It must have been a clean dive of two hundred feet. Both of them coming down made a noise like an approaching shell. The duck exploded the water and the peregrine was close enough to be smothered by the spray. I was sure it had followed the bird in, but not at all. An instant later it appeared veering away in level flight towards the trees. How it braked I shall never know. A minute later a duck mallard bobbed to the surface looking anxiously about but apparently none the worse for her stupendous dive. The last time I saw the peregrine at full speed it was tailing a grouse low across the moor and went over the horizon like a jet aeroplane, I think it was playing and not on a lethal hunt.

Today peregrines are on a slight increase after reaching a point of near extinction in the early 'sixties. Poison dressings stored by the seed eating pigeons which form 90 per cent of a peregrine's diet were the chief cause. Through eating quantities of the contaminated flesh of these birds peregrines slowly crippled themselves or became sterile. This blow to the peregrine population came at a time when it had just started to recover from the destruction of its eyries in the war for security reasons. I am sad to say that my position in the military world at the time made me partially implicated in this measure being undertaken in Scotland. I think it was a mistake because I doubt if their numbers even then warranted it, but in those dark days when the presence of German

U-boats ruled out any possibility of radio contact with our ships in the Atlantic, even the chance of losing one message-bearing pigeon for the sake of a bird seemed unacceptable beside the risk to human life.

Peregrines nest on coastal cliffs at sites, or eyries, that have been used in many cases since immemorial times. These days their numbers afford them territories extending probably as much as sixty miles in any direction. They never prey on birds in the immediate vicinity of their nest, often breeding above colonies of quite unruffled seabirds and rock doves. In Siberia they invariably nest with red-breasted geese because these birds are such efficient watchdogs. On the other hand peregrines will attack other birds of prey like the kestrel and merlin if the mood takes them. Similarly buzzards will attack an owl and an eagle a buzzard. Peregrines will also tackle their victims on the ground. If a grouse settles and squats in heather to evade a stoop, the peregrine is quite capable of settling and following the bird in under the clump. Unless they are very hungry they will not start eating immediately, and this is what made them such an admirable means of catching game birds for food before the gun was invented. They have no enemy other than man.

Shortly after I retired to the Borders from the army I had a call from a local keeper urging me to come as soon as I could to see this bird he had just shot. So I went, and there was a beautiful tiercel with a falconer's bell on its leg.

'God Andrew,' I said in dismay. 'Why did you shoot this lovely bird?'

'Well, Mr Henry, it's the only time in my life I've heard a bird ringing a bell so I shot it,' he explained with satisfaction.

We spent two months trying to find who owned this beautiful creature. But Andrew could not see his crime.

'You know all about birds,' he said. 'You ought to have told me some of them ring bells.'

The peregrine is not a common sight but its powerful shoulders and sharp wings make it unmistakable. It is the most aerial of the falcons and the fastest, faster than its northerly cousin the gyrfalcon, faster even than the sakers and lanners which are still the most treasured hunters of the desert sheikhs. One glorious May morning only two years ago I was waiting at Hirsel for a busload of birdwatchers when my eye was caught by a glint high overhead. I trained my field-glasses on it and there was a tiercel performing a series of intricate aerial manoeuvres, in which after a few minutes it was joined by its mate. These aerobatics undertaken at a height of 4000 feet were obviously being done for the sheer joy of flying; masterful and superb in the void of a cloudless summer sky. They were gone by the time the buses arrived.

## 6. | Game

As children my brothers and I were all brought up to shoot as a matter of course. I did not begin until I was about fourteen because my father was away at the War and he did not want me to start without him being there to teach me. Under his distant supervision I was an ornithologist long before I was ever a sportsman, although both hobbies seemed entirely compatible with the other. I looked forward no less eagerly to the first sight of swifts in May as to the first shot at a grouse on August 12. The timetable never changed. For the summer holidays we migrated to Douglas in Lanarkshire, hill country where our chief sport was grouse driving and rough, moorland shooting. Then at Christmas and Easter we were back in the arable Lowlands at Hirsel for the winter pheasant shoots, pigeon and duck flighting, the spring salmon fishing on Tweed and bird-watching. These pursuits involved us seven days a week, morning until dusk in all weathers, and from those years I think I have worked out a balance and philosophy applicable to any circumstance of human or other life.

On his return my father duly taught me the rudiments of shooting: how to avoid firing at horizons or where you could not see; how to unload before laying aside your gun; how not to point it at your neighbour by cradling it in your arms like a baby the way so many keepers do; how not to keep the safety catch on; how to direct your fire as unconsciously as if you were aiming a walking-stick. He showed us all this in two or three lessons pottering about the park, and then entrusted us to the care of a keeper for the rest of the holidays. Within a year we were as deadly as assassins.

Bird watching is a peaceful offspring of shooting. Few of the ornithologists I have known have not been shots and even fewer denied the importance of its part in making them the bird-lovers and experts they became. In the nineteenth century naturalists and specimen-hunters like St John only practised these rules as adjuncts to their shooting. They had to kill rarities to prove what they had seen. It is only in recent times that the specimen gun has made way for the camera and the tape-recorder. This long-established love of the chase has made the British the most conscientious people in Europe in their care of animals and birds, and the rituals of shooting have undoubtedly played their part. The dates of the various shooting seasons for various species were sacrosanct, and as bird-lovers we children recognised but never shot rarities and strictly observed a whole code of unwritten laws known to all countrymen: such as not to shoot patridges once they had paired, though this was usually two months before the official end of the season, or not to shoot hen pheasants after Christmas. Not only that, shooting also greatly extended our knowledge. Hiding in impenetrable thickets waiting for pigeons the length of a snowing winter afternoon teaches you more than any book.

Today shooting is big business to cover the vastly increased running costs, and an important source of income. There is a degree of competition about the numbers of pheasants required to entice valuable syndicates from one estate to another which was entirely lacking before the last War. The pheasant is the only gamebird which can be controlled in this way. There is no limit to the number you can rear on an estate if you feed them sufficiently. Estates which provided nicely balanced days of one hundred and fifty birds twenty years ago are now stocked to bursting point to offer syndicate shoots double-gun days and bags of thousands. I know of one which rears fifteen thousand birds – at the first shoot a fair proportion of these run between the guns like poultry.

The pheasant has suffered from the effects of rearing. The hens are now even more wayward mothers than they were before, having been brought up in anonymous incubators and pens. They desert easily, are unconcerned for their chicks and even lay their eggs in partridge nests by mistake. And yet rearing is not essential in producing large numbers. At Stetchworth near Newmarket they have never reared since the last War, yet they can shoot fifteen hundred birds on the opening day and still remove annually a large number of eggs to stock the sister estate in Berwickshire. The most extravagant way of avoiding all these hazards is to buy six-week old pullets from a game-farm, although they never seem to do well later. Experiments have been carried out with wing-tabs, which show that normally only 8 per cent of these birds are shot by the end of the season – a far lower return than for birds reared from the egg. Other gamebirds can be managed but all of them are too wild to withstand the husbandry to which the pheasant is agreeable.

There were pheasant 'battues' before but the motive for them was very different and there were far fewer of them. The ducal preserves of the Edwardian era vied for the honour of entertaining the King by providing the vast bags that were his delight and, of course, equally to the taste of the other great shots of the day – the de Greys and Harry Stonors – but the majority of estates hardly reared at all. An abundance of keepers controlled the vermin, and it was the growing science of keepering which really created the bags necessary to satisfy the demands of the much more deadly breechloading guns when these were introduced in the latter part of the nineteenth century. Keepering established a balance which could not have existed in the earlier predator dominated times. Anyone who doubts this need only take a train from Edinburgh to Glasgow, unkeepered country today in which you will be lucky to see anything but magpies and 'corbie' crows.

The gamebird most affected by the presence of game keepers was the red grouse. Far more territories were created for the birds in the breeding season and their numbers increased enormously as a result. A good grouse population depends on a moor managed to accommodate the maximum number of territories with the surplus birds being culled in the shooting season. Moors where the birds were shot in insufficient numbers fell foul of the traditional diseases and starvation (10 to 20 per cent in an average winter) and thus brought the healthy stock down with them. A good grouse stock is unproductive without shooting. To a lesser extent, because birds like blackgame and partridges have been more at the mercy of new techniques in farming and forestry, this is true of all gamebirds. It is equally true of animals. Since the decline of that maligned sport otter hunting, otters have found it very difficult to hold their own against river pollution without the protection that was ensured by the existence of the forces that controlled the sport. They are now a comparatively rare animal, and yet otter hunting is still derided. Fox hunting is pilloried just as ignorantly. The fur trade is the real threat to the continued existence of the fox. In 1977 a pelt retailed at an average of £14. Even with the protection afforded by the supervision of the hunts the fox population is falling alarmingly. Hunting is much less concerned with catching foxes than with the thrill of riding and the art of working hounds. Summers, huntsman of The Buccleuch for fifty years, had refined his art to such an extent that if no fox had appeared by three o'clock he could set his hounds off on the most hair-raising available line for home with one toot of his horn. Only the oldest followers knew there had been no fox involved when they all arrived conveniently at kennels by dusk and a welcome in the Buccleuch Arms.

The First War created a vacuum in rural affairs. Men and often the money were absent but there were still a few figures left to embody the professional attitude to shooting and the other country pursuits of the Edwardian élite. One June morning in the early thirties when I was working in an office in Berkeley Square, I was summoned by my uncle Brackley – Lord Ellesmere – to have a drink at his palatial residence in St James's, Bridgewater House. I arrived about 11 o'clock to find him and the butler dodging about behind a pile of furniture practising the art of loading with two guns: a one hour exercise they performed every day throughout the summer to keep in trim for the shooting season ahead.

Much the largest of gamebirds, and the largest bird in Britain today in the absence of the great bustard, is the capercailzie. It used to be indigenous to this country as fossils have shown, but with the gradual felling of the Caledonian Forest its habitat slowly disappeared so that by the nineteenth century it was declared extinct. Later it was reintroduced from Sweden by Lord Breadalbane and has flourished in north-east Scotland ever since. With time the huge new plantations of the Forestry Commission should greatly increase its distribution, perhaps beyond its ancenstral range. In Europe one of the most prized sports is to stalk the cock when it gives its love call from the top of a spruce tree. During this ecstasy the bird is oblivious to the world but every few seconds he stops suddenly to observe the effect of his efforts on the females in the vicinity. They are usually attracted to the foot of the tree and if he sees one he will pop down and mate. You must stalk closer only when he is blind to your movements during this song. The slightest sound or movement in between and the game will be over, but if the stalker's fieldcraft is good enough, an hour of tiptoeing will be rewarded by the chance of a shot with a rifle. In Norway I remember people gambled like mad on the outcome. Here the birds are usually driven out of the woods like pheasants.

All the gamebirds have a strict territorial sense and are markedly sedentary. At the turn of the century there was a red grouse at Cawdor in Aberdeenshire, which the keeper had tamed. During the shooting season it would entertain the guests by walking up and down the dining-room table at breakfast, taking an occasional peck at a plate and calling 'Go Back! Go Back!' at the house party, who would be about to set off for a day's grouse driving. One year the moor was taken by an Englishman who completely fell in love with the bird and succeeded in bribing its owner to part with it. The grouse was packed in a hamper and sent by train five hundred miles south to Henley-on-Thames. There everything continued happily until one morning two weeks later it was discovered that the bird was missing from its pen. The new owner was desperate but after a day or two of frantic searching he decided that a cat must have eaten it, so he wrote to the keeper at Cawdor to break the sad news. The keeper wrote back to say the bird had beaten the Englishman's letter north by a day. Grouse have no migratorial ambitions but apparently they have a homing instinct.

On some days, grouse vacate moors altogether, yet when this happens adjoining moors never report equivalent increases. This ability of theirs to vanish was demonstrated for me at Douglas by an albino. The bird inhabited a very flat part of the hill where the view was uninterrupted. Three consecutive drives all took place on this great downward sweep of moorland: the first drove the birds on to the lower ground, then the lower ground was driven back towards the first drive and finally the first drive was beaten out again over a different line of butts. At every shoot for eight years this albino appeared at the first and third drives but never in the second. How it succeeded in returning to its first position without detection, looking as it did as bright as a flanker's flag, remains a mystery. It was never fired at and in its ninth year a keeper found it dead on the hill, sliced through by a peregrine.

Such independence makes the grouse an impossible bird to control, although attempts to rear it continue and a pellet has been devised that can be fed to it in captivity. As yet, however, reared birds cannot be weaned of this artificial food, and they never lose their fierce territorial instincts. There was a famous hand-reared bird at Tomintoul. It was entirely dependent on the keeper for food but as a mature bird it assumed territorial control of a few acres of ground beyond the burn opposite his cottage. With the exception of its foster-parent it even refused humans admission to this territory. The local postman, who was daily thrown from his bicycle by its attacks, was eventually issued with a mini by the Council as protection. All this soon came to the attention of the B.B.C. and it was not long before I found myself going north for combat duty with 'Old Jock', as the bird had by then affectionately come to be known. There I was early one miserably wet morning with grouse, one of which I assumed to be my antagonist, cailing all around, and a keeper who was giving me final orders. The chances of success seemed very forlorn.

'You wait till you've crossed that burn,' said the keeper.

'I shall,' I said stoically, fed up already with the mist and bitter cold.

He was absolutely right. No sooner was I over than this grouse whirred up out of the beyond crying 'Go Back! Go Back!' and made a stab at my face. I buried my head and beat a stumbling retreat. As soon as I was over the water it left off and stood furiously to attention on a look-out rock, grunting and fanning its tail as a warning against my making any further advances. We got some wonderful recordings. Eventually I asked if it could also be induced to make the territorial call: a lovely bubbling crescendo usually uttered as the birds cavort a few feet into the air above a chosen spot.

'Well,' the keeper explained, 'it's just a matter of jerking a handkerchief at it.'

'What about you doing it?' I suggested hopefully.

'You'll be fine, you'll be fine.'

So I went over the burn again. Old Jock came winging up as before and when I had weathered his first thrusts he dropped to the ground at my feet and I quickly relaxed my fist to release the concealed handerkerchief. Hardly had I had time to give it the prescribed jerk before he sprang up like a fighting cock. My arm was raised and I clamped him to my ribs. Grouse are not small but luckily, unlike cock pheasants, they have no spurs on the backs of the legs.

'Well here I am with Old Jock under my arm,' I reported as calmly as I could into the mike. He was raking my sleeve with his claws and pecking viciously. 'When I release him,' I continued struggling to keep a hold of him, 'we should hear him make the bubbling call we just talked about'.

And to my amazement he obliged. Afterwards as I recovered my breath on the other side of the burn the sound-engineers came on the line:

'I wonder if you could do that again Henry. We got the tone wrong.' But their ill-concealed mirth gave the game away.

I did not see Old Jock again, but I understand the keepers played a dirty trick on him one day. They took him out grouse-driving and when he was released from his gamebag he jumped on to the nearest butt and gave the unsuspecting occupant such hell that he hardly dared fire a shot for the rest of the day. Old Jock meanwhile flew back to his domain by the burn and was still muttering with fury when the keeper returned in the evening.

Grouse are monogamous though the male is not an over attentive father. They nest in tall heather and have agile chicks which are fully capable of flight within a week of hatching.

Their sinuous ability in the air and explosive speed off the ground make them relatively safe from all predators except the rare peregrine. It is the scavengers which do most damage. Carrion crows will reduce an unkeepered moor to a few old pairs by stealing all the eggs. As sporting birds grouse are unrivalled, providing a faster and more variable target than any other gamebird, but shooting them is also notoriously dangerous in consequence.

The last time I ever shot was at grouse, and made appropriately memorable for me by the presence of a foreign ambassador. It was rumoured that he was a star marksman in his own country so we all looked forward to see how he measured up to this ultimate test. At the first drive he had drawn a butt in the middle of the line between an old family friend, Willie Hill-Wood, and the late Lord Salisbury. I was next to Willie and Alec was beyond me. The drive began and I was firing away gaily when suddenly Alec roared out: 'What the hell are Willie and Bobbity up to?' Birds were streaming over their positions and there was no sign of either of them. The ambassador on the other hand seemed to be having a whale of a time. At the end of the drive they reappeared. Alec came down the line in a most un-characteristic rage. 'What the devil were you up to Willie?' Willie and Bobbity on the other hand looked ashen. Apparently the ambassador's shooting had forced them undercover and they now refused to continue if they had to be next to him. As Alec was Foreign Secretary at the time this was an extremely awkward ultimatum, however I could see he was seeking a peace formula. Little did I suspect what it was. 'We're going to alter the draw,' he announced eventually, without explanation to the party in general. 'Henry and I will be changing numbers with Willie and Bobbity!'

Why the ambassador spared us I shall never know. It must have been Alec's diplomatic immunity.

Where there are red grouse there will probably also be black grouse or blackgame. The most notorious fact about blackgame is their habit of mating only on special 'lekking' grounds. Leks are normally sited on little patches or knolls of grass in the heather, and here the cocks congregate to show off their superbly heraldic plumage to the nondescript greyhens which enter the lek in turn to be trod by one or more of the disporting males. The restrictiveness of lekking has its disadvantages: an old greyhen may dominate the ground and refuse entry to her younger rivals or, as happened at Douglas, cock pheasants may take advantage of their spurs to chase the blackcock off. After mating the greyhen retires to lay her eggs and raise her young without any further contact with her mate until the next breeding season.

The habitat of blackgame in these days of mechanisation and efficiency has suffered almost as much as that of the quail and, to a lesser degree, the partridge. The uniform planting of conifers and the deep drains cut into so much hill ground by the new machines have greatly reduced its numbers. Deep drains should always contain escape routes to enable the trapped chicks of hill nesters, waders as well as grouse, to climb out once they have fallen in. Thousands of fledglings are lost this way every spring as they endeavour to follow their mothers across the maze of a newly cut slope. It is difficult to see how the pattern of this decline can be changed.

Up on the hill at Douglas there were also the moorland partridges, so hardy as to almost qualify as a different species from their lowland counterparts. Partridges too are very aggressive territorially and, as with grouse, old birds and barren pairs should be shot if the nesting ratio per acre is to be increased; young cocks are much less cantankerous and prepared to settle for smaller domains. The hens are as tenacious parents as any duck and the cocks are uniquely co-operative, grey partridges often sharing the incubation of the eggs and cock red legs even incubating a second clutch while the hen hatches the first: a method which has undoubtedly contributed to the growth of their numbers in England ever since their introduction in the last century.

Although unrelated, partridges can often be confused with corncrakes. Like all the rails, corncrakes are very unwilling flyers, trailing along weakly for fifty yards and then pitching clumsily into barley or rushes never to be seen again – even if you try to hunt them out with a dog. Yet, astonishingly, all the British breeding population migrates from Africa. Fifty years ago at Hirsel I remember being kept awake by the incessant grating of their calls through the summer nights but, like partridges, they are very much reduced in numbers. The turnover from hay to sileage has been disastrous for them. Hundreds of unsuspecting crakes must have been minced by the cutters now that the long grass is no longer required to grow into protective hay, and increasingly the bird has been driven to the fringes of the moors. You will rarely see them but their call – like the teeth of a comb being thumbed – is unmistakably resonant and loud. All birds must make this contact with a rival. If they do not they will not rest long. It is like a club. A man would never join a club if he was the only member, and most birds are no less gregarious. Corncrakes also have an astonishing ability to throw their voices. If you record one you will usually find that after a few minutes the call is coming from eighty yards behind you rather than twenty yards in front, but when you move towards this new position you will realise that the sound is still coming from where you first supposed. How they do this is a mystery but in some way they appear to be able to bounce sound off objects, particularly stone walls, so that a confusion of echoes is created which soon leaves an unfortunate listener bemused.

Quails are different from all the other British gamebirds in that they migrate to us from Africa for the summer. In this and its habitat it too resembles the corncrake, but its decline has been even more marked. The last fifty years have seen its numbers fall so disastrously that it now has the status in Britain of a rare bird. The blame for this can be attributed largely to the Arabs and Italians who discovered that there was a vast fortune to be amassed by killing and selling quails as a luxury food, mist nets

sometimes stretching a hundred miles being erected to catch the
exhausted birds on their migrations. Then, in 1931, Mussolini
made a law banning the trapping of migrating quails in Italy.
The Arabs continued, but this one statute must have saved
millions of the birds over the years. To show just how many it is
only necessary to look at a nineteenth-century game book. In
the columns assigned to the various species the quail ranks
second in importance to the pheasant. After 1900 the column is
not only demoted but slowly discarded. Before Mussolini's law
a 'good' year saw as much as 80 per cent of the North African
quail population destroyed as it passed through Italy. Now,
unbelievably, the Italians have revoked the law.

A few descendants of the ancient hordes sometimes turn up in
Scotland. Three years ago my brother Edward telephoned to say
he had shot one. It was tipped in the wing having apparently
aligned itself with a snipe which Edward had missed – a rare
enough event in itself – and if it had not been retrieved by his
dog he would never have known of its existence. He brought it
over for my aviary, and when I was in Malta during a lecture
tour the following year I bought it a male companion from a
bird-seller in Valetta. I often restock my aviaries by buying
abroad and this time was no exception, so I had a selection of
canaries as well as the quail when the time came for my customs
declaration at Southampton. Everything went as smoothly as
usual until I came to the end of my list with the words 'and one
male quail'.

'What!' exclaimed the customs man. 'A quail . . .'

'Yes, a quail. You know Q.U.A. . . .'

'Can't do that.'

It had been a long voyage and we were in a hurry to get
home. It was utterly exasperating. He sent for the superintendent,
a pompous fat ass who produced a list a yard long. 'I hear
you've got a quail?'

'Yes, I've got forty canaries and one male quail.'

'Can't let you through with that, sir.'

'One male quail!'

'There's a very strict order, I think signed by your brother, saying no importation of quails allowed, No. we've had to clamp down on that because there's a terrible market between Italy and the U.K. How do we know you're not going to sell it as food? We'll have to detain it I'm afraid sir.'

'Look here my dear fellow, I don't care a damn about that. This is *one* quail.'

'That's where the rot sets in. You bring in one and the next person'll bring in a hundred.'

The anomaly still exists. It took one and a half hours to get through, we missed all our connections and when we at last got home we discovered Edward's female had died anyway!

There is nothing new in the persecution of quails. Scholars have suggested that the 'manna from Heaven' which saved the Jews from starving in the desert was an equally lost and exhausted migration of the bird. I think they are right.

I have left the pheasant till last because everyone knows it, but in my lectures I have found that surprisingly few people know that by nature it is really a marsh bird. Cock pheasants in particular are quite strong swimmers. Only with the rise of its sporting popularity has it been forced to breed and live in woods. Pheasants are legendarily supposed to have been imported into England by the Romans but, whatever happened before, it was not until the 1820's that they were introduced at Hirsel and on one or two other Scottish estates, where they have thrived ever since. Today their numbers are quite disproportionate owing to the commercialisation of shooting.

You can soon tell their numbers in a neighbourhood. Any sudden atmospheric bump or tremor offends their ear-drums and sets all the cocks crowing for miles whatever the time of day. It is said that the earliest news of the Battle of Jutland in the First War was derived from the agitation of the pheasants in East Anglia. They sensed the shock waves from the discharges of the great naval guns out in the North Sea, inaudible as a sound to human ears.

When I was broadcasting in 1976 I met the zoologist Cherry Bramble, a great expert on bats. One of her pets was a fruit bat, which she often wore at her neck where it hung from the shoulders of her dress by two suitably positioned hooks. She had derived a lot of amusement from carrying it in this way when out shopping. But one thing puzzled her and that was the effect it had on her baby. If the bat was in the room the child would often scream. Eventually she realised that the infant was being driven demented by the pitch of the bat's cries which to Cherry's less sensitive adult hearing remained totally inaudible.

Pheasants rarely move more than five miles from where they have been reared and usually stay in their home wood. This makes them especially vulnerable to poachers.

I have experienced poachers both at Douglas and Hirsel but none of them has been more artful than my eldest stepson Christopher Wills. One holiday when he was a boy I showed him the exact boundaries of my 300-acre farm, although, despite his protestations of ignorance, I knew he knew them better than I did. In the course of the next few hours I was telephoned in turn by all of my adjoining neighbours protesting that they had been poached by some boy who said he was my stepson, and that I had told him that he could shoot anywhere because I owned all the land between my house and the Border, roughly one hundred square miles!

# 7. | *Douglas and waders*

Every August we travelled eighty miles west of Hirsel to spend
the summer holidays at Douglas in Lanarkshire. Douglas was an
entirely different landscape of moors, burns, little villages and
occasional cropping. It was a windy change from the lush fields
and woods of Hirsel and more sparse in the variety of its bird life.
This is generally typical of Western Britain. The great majority
of our migrating birds spread south and north from the European
highway. The west coast is off the route and on the whole too
barren and windswept to draw across the woodland species in
any numbers. But Douglas nevertheless provided me with the
opportunity to see several species and families of bird I rarely, if
ever, saw at Hirsel. There were red grouse and blackgame, of
course, the west coast wildfowl like the bean goose and merganser,

the peregrine and most variously, an abundance of hill waders, notably the greenshank.

Waders are transformed in appearance by their breeding plumage. We never see the grey plover in its glory because it nests to the north of Britain and its cousin the golden plover has largely migrated or disappeared to the moors by the time its white chest has turned to glistening black; and the same is true of most of those small species which flicker anonymously along the tidelines throughout the autumn and winter months. Some years ago a small bird was brought to me which had been shot on Greenlaw Moor in mistake for a snipe. I was not sure what the bird was so I sent it up to the Royal Scottish Museum in Edinburgh for their more expert opinion. They had it a month and compared it with every possible skin in the collection before coming to the conclusion that it was nothing more unusual than an immature male dunlin. In breeding plumage it would have been identifiable through binoculars at hundreds of yards.

One August day in 1926 I made a solitary expedition at Douglas to shoot snipe, and when I settled down to my sandwich lunch I noticed a much bigger bird among the dozen or so that I had tipped out on to the heather. This was a great snipe, at that time only the forty-fourth to have been officially recorded in Scotland. Great snipe probably were then, and certainly are now, commoner birds than the records suggested, and with experience I recognised several over the years. As with so many rarities, if you know what you are looking for you are much more likely to see it.

Except in the breeding season, snipe are generally secretive birds. They feed most of the day under cover and then, like duck, flight on to more open ground at dusk. It will usually be too dark to see them, but you will hear a swish and a 'plop' as they land in the shallows and, if you are near enough, the sucking noises of their feeding as they withdraw their long beaks from the mud. On one occasion I brought one home that had damaged the top joint of its wing against a fence wire. I had no experience of keeping the birds, but as soon as I arrived I asked Collingwood to bring a footbath up to my bedroom while I went out and cut some turfs. He was a bit surprised, but it all proved a great success. I laid the turfs out on the bottom of the footbath, filled it until they were half submerged and left the bird standing forlornly on top as I went off to have a wash. When I got back there were the most wonderful noises of sucking from the footbath, and there was the snipe using the suction pipe of his beak for all he was worth as the worms oozed to the surface of the waterlogged earth. I have never known a wild bird adjust so quickly to captivity, and it convinced me that they would make admirable pets if you could satisfy their hunger. It lived long enough to demonstrate that it could eat as many as ten large worms in an equal number of minutes: an exceptional bird, not least for the composure it showed after being jostled the five miles home in my pocket.

Spring is the best time to see them. If you go to any moor in April and May you will soon distinguish a noise like the bleating of lambs coming from the sky. This is the 'drumming' of the snipe: a love flight in which the male bird rises to a height and then planes down, letting the wind vibrate the two outside feathers of his tail to produce this odd, very resonant sound. Then the male will alight on a prominence and give a squeaking call of reassurance to his mate before flying off to continue his ecstatic display over the breeding area. Usually there are several birds doing it in the air at once, and I have heard it as late as August if the weather is balmy. A controversy raged for years over whether the sound was vocal or mechanical, but the nature of it can be easily demonstrated if you stick two stiff chicken feathers either side of a cork and give it a whirl.

The snipe is another bird much valued by sportsmen for the testing speed and indirection of its flight, and the sharpness of its flavour. Snipe are as fast as any bird on take off and should always be walked down wind if they are to be shot successfully. People invariably walk them up wind because they think the snipe will hear less and sit tighter; but the real problem is to see the bird, and as they always rise into wind a momentary flash of their white chests will be offered to a down-wind walker. I long ago came to the conclusion that they were really too small to warrant shooting.

In the autumn, resident birds are joined by large numbers of migrants from northern Europe. Snipe not only frequent water-logged ground. In August and September I have often seen them on very dry, barren stretches of hill pasture, but this is the exception. They seldom go down to the sea.

If you disturb a snipe it will rise high into the air and fly out of sight; the jack snipe will skim the rushes like a butterfly and re-settle within eighty yards at the most. And yet this tiny bird migrates to us for the winter from far farther north than almost any other species, so far north that its nest was not discovered until 1908. How they survive the buffeting of such a long, often oceanic journey is a marvel. They are not a bird of the open marshes, but usually settle down in a favourite patch of rushes in the corner of a field. These patches are not selected at random but appear to be almost an inheritance, because if the resident jack snipe is shot (a pointless activity because they really are only a mouthful) another one will have taken its place within a day, although no jack snipe may inhabit similar patches of rushes for a mile around.

Experts say that it is only in the last hundred years that wood-cock have become resident in any numbers in this country. They claim that until then they were only a winter migrant. I find this very difficult to believe, because conditions now are far less agreeable to them than they were then in an age of woods and bogs. Today they are certainly common residents, and this home population is bolstered, as with the snipe, by large 'falls' from Scandinavia and the Baltic in the autumn. These migrations can be vast. An old admiral once told me that when he was the captain of a destroyer patrolling the North Sea off Denmark in the First War, a lot of birds came on to his ship one night during a westerly gale. He posted a rating to investigate and the man returned with two handfuls of woodcock. There was another destroyer lying not far off to windward so, no doubt highly improperly, the captain signalled: 'Shine search lights. Inundated with woodcock'. Both ships then played their lights on the intervening stretch of sea and the waves were brown with the birds. Being very partial to roast woodcock the captain had no hesitation, despite the swell, in ordering boats to be lowered and these salvaged at least 300 of the drowned birds. Even so, this represented only a sample of those lying within the beams of the searchlights. Who knows what numbers were floating in the darkness beyond? Such losses may be more usual than we think.

Woodcock are just as secretive as the other snipe, their large eyes betraying their nocturnal preference. They are the most woodland of waterbirds, lying up undercover, usually in bracken by day and flighting out to feed at dusk. Much the best time to see them is in the breeding season when the mates will beat the bounds of, or 'rode' (the Scandinavian equivalent), their territories in the twilight on special flights. Roding is stylised by slow, considered wingbeats, rather like an owl's and a wispy call, followed by three faint grunts, which is repeated at regular intervals. The circuit does not take long to complete, so if a woodcock passes overhead it will reappear within five minutes if you are prepared to wait, and may continue roding in this way for up to an hour. Then it will descend in the dark to rejoin the nesting female. Woodcock are March nesters and will sometimes produce four broods in a season. I have seen chicks as late as September. The female sits very tight and is so well camouflaged that against a coppery background of dead leaves the thing that most usually gives her away is the liquid black drop of her eye. My brother George one day reported that he had found a woodcock's nest. He had marked it by planting a stick so I went down to have a look. I followed instructions, found the stick and up clattered a mallard, exposing a clutch of ten eggs.

'You damned fool,' I said when I got back. 'Surely you know the difference between a mallard's and a woodcock's nest. I've been all that way for nothing.'

'Nonsense, my dear fellow, there's a woodcock's nest within three feet of that stick. Perhaps you should get some spectacles.'

So we both went down to look under this wellingtonia tree, each one convinced he was right, and there within two feet of the mallard's nest was a woodcock sitting on hers. George was thrilled. Two birds of different species will often nest beside each other like this, it is only when they are of the same species that the trouble usually starts. The sheltered ground at the root of a wellingtonia is always a likely place for a woodcock to nest.

Another feature of their behaviour is the ability to carry the young in flight. This is now accepted as ornithological fact, but it has never been photographed. I have witnessed it several times but never more spectacularly than at Hirsel in the summer of 1974 when, along with a party of thirty-two birdwatchers and experts, from a bridge over the Leet I watched a female pick up each of her brood of three in turn and carry them, gripped between her thighs and supported by her tail, across the river below. Before we could stop him a little boy in the party ran down, disturbing the mother away, and carried one of the chicks back to its original position on the other bank. Dr Ian Meikle agreed to allow the experiment to proceed but insisted that only the boy and two others of the party should remain. They rejoined us shortly afterwards in a great state of excitement at having seen the female perform the operation a third time. Needless to say, I think this was the only occasion when not one member of a tour had a camera. Usually people are bristling with them, and even cines. As a film it would have been historic.

Undoubtedly the most easily and frequently seen of all the wading birds is the green plover or peewit. Peewits flock winter pastures and nest on both rough and arable land in the spring, circling and tumbling on broad, clubbed wings. The egg is considered a great delicacy, though I defy anyone to differentiate its taste from that of a jackdaw or waterhen, and can be gathered for your own consumption in this country until April 15. Abroad their numbers still allow this to be done commercially, as with the black-headed gull here and elsewhere. The nest is a scrape on heathland or, most commonly, harrowed plough, and can best be detected by surveying a field through binoculars and charting the positions of the sitting birds, rather than laboriously quartering the ground looking at your feet. In the old days a ploughman walking behind his horse-drawn harrow would see the peewits leave the nest and lift the eggs out of the way, something the bird does not mind at all, whereas nowadays too many tractormen have not the time, interest or even knowledge of the countryside to bother with such niceties. But perhaps there will be a change of attitude. After a recent broadcast in which I had deplored the loss of such old countrymen I was delighted to be told by two farmers in my home district that they and their tractormen always stopped to move the nests. In fact one said he had lifted sixteen in a single field and not one bird had deserted. I wish I could think such husbandry was more widespread but the folly of intensive farming seems to continue unabated. Few modern agriculturists seem to think; they just go on. It is a lack of awareness rather than of knowledge, a lack of awareness of the future effects of their actions and of the importance of keeping nature alive. Too few seem to realise that if you extend a field by taking away an old hedge, you will also let in the wind and snow; that if you plough too deep and often, you will thin the soil; that most poisons once released take decades to be broken down. The peewits, thanks to stringent protection laws, have held their own and survived the incredible agricultural revolution since the War. Forty years ago, when there were no tractors, the peewit could bring up its first brood completely undisturbed. Now with the loss of so much rough pasture, which provided the majority of its feeding, it has learned to adapt to our folly.

Peewits are usually thought of in conjunction with the larger, curved beaked curlews. Curlews have also found it increasingly hard to survive on modern farms, their favourite nesting sites being the bogs and rushes which used to exist in so many field bottoms before the War. Nowadays it is much more of an upland bird, and more of a seabird in the winter than the peewit. Sometimes they succeed in adjusting to the disturbance of a particular field – a pair nested in the middle of one of mine for several seasons – but in general they are one of the wariest of birds, the watchdogs for all other species. Partly this is due to their high stature, partly to their remarkable powers of sight and the strength of their alarm call. Curlews will be voicing this alarm as soon as you come within a quarter of a mile of them, and every other bird in the vicinity will thus be alerted to your presence whether they can see you or not. Female curlews on the nest, however, will sit almost as close as woodcock. There were two ancient men in Lanarkshire in my youth who lived out in the hills, about twenty miles from anywhere, both great birdmen; one a shepherd the other our keeper. One spring the shepherd saw an extraordinary thing, an albino curlew sitting on eggs, so he took the trouble – no trouble really with a good swig of whisky every half-mile – to trudge over into the next valley and report his discovery to his old friend, my father's head keeper. Four days later the keeper duly called by and after yet another dram they went down onto the field to take a look at the bird. And the keeper had a great laugh, because the white bird on the hillside turned out to be an albino peewit. He gave the shepherd an awful ribbing for not knowing the difference and the shepherd had to take it, although he could not understand what had happened. Anyway they had another bottle of whisky, and when they went out to have a last look before the old keeper tottered off home, they both thought they were seeing double because the albino curlew had returned to its nest alongside the albino peewit.

If you see peewits in a field it is always worth looking for the smaller, thrushlike, golden plover. On the wing it is not thrush-like at all of course, gathering into swift packs of up to five hundred birds which flicker about the sky in the characteristic fashion of so many of the smaller waders. In spring most breeding pairs take to the moors. All the inland waders have lovely calls and at the edge of a moor on a May evening the air will be full of the bubbling calls of curlews, the wispy notes of the peewits and the clear pipes of the golden plover.

Golden Plover are strangely approachable birds, despite their aerobatic flying, especially if you want to play tricks. One of the easiest ways to attract them is to walk through the field with a yellow dog, ideally a golden labrador. The resident flock of goldens will come running after you but not, for some strange reason, if you have a black dog. No less appealing is their reaction if you perform the grass pulling trick. When you come into the field you bend over and snatch a tag of long grass from the side of the dyke or fence, and then purposively walk off in the opposite direction to the flock. But every now and then you pretend to pick more grass and each time you do it you adjust your course so that you slowly come full circle to the birds. Again for some reason they are transfixed by this behaviour, all looking wonderingly as if to say: 'Stupid old fool, what's he doing picking rushes for?' Until to their surpise you are not a distant figure but an awesome danger only twenty yards away.

This way of bamboozling birds and animals by distracting their attention is often used by stoats. A stoat will slink through the grass, sleek as a snake, and then directly it comes into the arena of its quarry it will start preening itself, displaying its white-front and generally behaving as if it had not an evil thought in its head. All the rabbits – it normally does not work if there are only two or three – will look on in a state of fascinated bewilderment. And all the time the stoat will edge deeper and deeper into the warren or the field until, with an electrifying leap, he will be at the throat of his victim. The other rabbits think this is terrible and dive underground immediately, and yet half-an-hour later when they are all out feeding again, the female stoat will come by and kill another one by exactly the same method. Stoats will also pretend to throw fits to disarm birds – jumping, twisting, rolling and contorting themselves dementedly until, with a final gigantic leap, they will land on the puzzled, immobilised onlooker.

The other legendary habit of stoats is to congregate into large numbers when they are on the move, something they do more frequently in moorland areas. There are several well-authenticated tales from the nineteenth century of people returning home late at night, no doubt a bit worse for drink, who were found severely bitten or even chewed to death in the morning having unwisely disputed the right of way with a horde of stoats. I do not doubt the truth of such horror stories. I once found a stoat at a pigeon I had shot, which refused to leave off its sucking and, in the ensuing tustle for the bird, went for my throat too. I kicked it to the ground and it slunk away, but it left me in no doubt of its intentions. The head keeper at Douglas was up feeding pheasants one Sunday with one of the under-keepers in the ride of a conifer plantation, always a likely route for stoat migrations, and they suddenly became aware of the animals creeping through the heather all around them. The head keeper had once been bitten by one so he got out quick.

'We'll fetch a gun,' he said jumping on his bicycle.

'But it's Sunday,' protested the under-keeper.

'Bugger that!' Thundered the older man peddling off for all he was worth.

They returned in time to shoot thirty-three. I have never seen more than thirty on the trot at one time, but even then I was happier to steer clear. They will not attack unless their path is blocked but if it is, and there are enough of them, even a man with a gun would be well advised to step aside.

## 8. | Gulls

Some birds have thrived and greatly increased during my lifetime and there have been miraculous and unexplained extensions of the breeding grounds of two species, the collared dove from the Bosphorous and the fulmars from St Kilda. I was first notified in 1952 of the arrival of a collared dove in this country. In those days its rarity meant that only ornithological circles were informed in case, by telling the public, it might be frightened away! Little did we realise that only twenty-five years later it would be shot quite legitimately as a pest. It bred at Hirsel for the first time in 1958, has colonised Ireland and now even comes aboard ships in mid-Atlantic. Obviously one day it will reach America. There has never been such a rapid expansion, both of range and numbers, of a single species in the history of ornithology and no one has a scientific explanation for it.

If it were not for the fulmar immediately disproving my

theory, I would suggest that birds, like mankind, tend to expand westwards. But the unique colony of fulmars on St Kilda has colonised most of the suitable coastal cliffs of mainland Britain by moving east. Again there is no scientific explanation. Could it be that in the absence of the islanders, who pickled and cured great numbers of fulmar eggs and birds each summer as a winter food supply, the colony slowly grew too large and had to expand to survive?

*Fulmars*

P.S.

Increases in resident species are usually due to our providing the food which enables more of them to live. Birds are very quick to make the most of these opportunities and often reveal remarkable powers of intercommunication and organised adaptability in the process. Eight thousand pochard, almost the entire British winter population of the bird, gathered on Duddingston Loch, within the city limits of Edinburgh, for over a month in the early spring of 1976, undoubtedly attracted by something peculiarly appetising in the water. If a certain part of a moor suffers a plague of voles, large number of short-eared owls will take advantage of the increase by coming in from miles around and settling down to hunt and nest in numbers large enough to form a loose-knit owlery. I have seen a hundred pairs on a moor at such times and to reap the full benefits of the glut, clutches will often be spontaneously increased from the average six, to twelve and even sixteen eggs. In this way the local short-eared population can rapidly be doubled, offsetting the losses they sustain from starvation when voles are scarce. Woodpigeons reach their nesting peak in the autumn during the corn harvest for the same reason, and the Australian diamond doves in my aviary proved how genetic these instincts can be by rearing six broods in accordance with the natural food cycle of the Antipodes. Sewage works, gravel pits, aerodromes and motorways have all benefited birds, and electricity has created the warm, metropolitan roosts of starlings and pigeons, but no family has capitalised more successfully on such innovations than the gulls.

In my youth you rarely saw a gull inland outside the breeding season, but rubbish dumps, gravel pits and mechanised farming have changed all that. Today large numbers of herring, black-headed and common gulls could quite accurately be described as land birds. Most herring gulls now eat as much garbage as fish guts. On Tweed they also benefited from the large numbers of dead salmon killed by the epidemics of disease in the mid-sixties, but they remain coastal nesters. Black-headed and common gulls are the main benefactors of mechanised farming. Until 1960 there was pasture with occasional plough in the Borders, now there is plough with occasional pasture, and the pattern is the same elsewhere. Both birds have had a feast.

I have only once seen a common gull nest in Berwickshire – as noticeable as a snowball in the middle of a thirty-acre field harrowed ready for sowing. Like black-headeds they are inland nesters but the common prefers to breed in small deserted colonies, often on islets among the lochs of the north west of Scotland, whereas the black-headed is a ubiquitous bog coloniser. There is a famous colony in Peebleshire alongside the busy A68, and in Berwickshire an equally long-established site at Bemersyde. These species have always come inland to nest but whereas in the old days they used then to return to the coast, many of them now probably remain on the land throughout their lives.

In my opinion gulls are the most difficult birds of all to identify. The reason for this is the length of time it takes for all species to achieve their extremely similar adult plumages, the time varying in ratio to their size from two to five years. Even the colours of their legs change during this period, one of the most reliable ways of differentiating adult gulls outside the breeding season. The common gull, for instance, is best distinguished in winter from the red legged black-headeds by its yellow legs, and so on.

One winter day it was reported to me that there was a Ross's gull with a flock of black-headeds on the Tweed at Kelso. Ross's is an Arctic bird so I was well prepared to be disappointed. It turned out to be an albino black-headed, easily told by its red albino eye and red legs. As usual various locals came forward as soon as they heard of my interest to say they had wondered what it was for over a year and from them I learned that it had disappeared the previous summer. I assumed it went to the nearest colony, in this case the one at Bemersyde, so when summer came I went up there to see if I could find it, but it was useless. Having splashed about the tussocks in a snowstorm of gulls and droppings I gave up in despair. Bogs are not to be entered into lightly. The tussocks make them look shallow whereas they are in fact full of holes deep enough to drown you. Gulls eggs are thought a great delicacy and by commercially culling Bemersyde, which must contain five thousand nests at least, its owner Lord Haig can potentially lift forty thousand eggs without doing the gulls any harm at all. If one egg is left and each nest lifted of new eggs every four days until the birds stop laying, quite enough eggs will hatch to maintain the colony, and a substantial income will be made without the cost of any initial investment at all. The only problem is the arduous work of gathering the crop. Such culling is, if anything, beneficial. In the great bird sanctuary on the Isle of May herring and lesser black-backed gulls have to be culled to preserve the colonies of frailer birds like terns.

In the last War every palatable egg available was used, especially those of the kittywake, but herring gulls' as well. I was lucky enough to visit the Orkneys a lot, where there was no rationing. All the spare space on the ships was used to carry ammunition and replacement parts to and from the Fleet in Scapa Flow, so that there was no way of exporting the produce of the island. I never saw such food: lobsters, crabs, salmon, every variety of sea fish, mutton, lamb, beef and two million hens. There was an absolute glut of hens' eggs, something which was an extreme luxury on the mainland, and I used to travel home by air weighed down with gifts like a Father Christmas. They literally could not get rid of the stuff. Islands are great places in times of war, pestilence and famine. And often they are very good for seeing birds too.

Needless to say there was at least one disaster involving all these elements of egg cropping, war and islands. It involved a tiny rock in the Firth of Forth called Inchmiceray which had been transformed into a gun battery. For ornithologists it was a shrine: the only place in Scotland where you could find a large breeding colony of roseate terns. The silent gun battery did not worry them in the least and in fact with the military police vetting each visitor to the island, however grand, they were better protected under the army from the ravages of vermin and egg collectors than ever before or since. But after the War the time soon came for the army to move out. Naturally they sold off all the equipment and nissen huts, and these were bought by a friend of mine in Edinburgh, Commander Donald Ross. Donald was a great businessman. He owned the smartest restaurant in Edinburgh, 'L'Aperitif', and was always buying up odd military stores and selling them at a vast profit. So he bought everything that was going on Inchmiceray and carted it off in two boats. One day about a fortnight after this exercise was under way Ian Pitman came up to me in a state at 'L'Aperitif': 'Have you seen? Well go and look at the bar. It's too serious for words!' Donald, not knowing the difference between a roseate tern egg and an ostrich's but having an eye as sharp as a herring gull's for a quick profit, had picked up and boiled every single egg on the island and was selling them off in basketfulls at the restaurant. There were at least twenty dozen, a terrible sight. I went straight off to beard him in his office.

'Look here, you'd better get these "gulls" eggs off the bar pretty quick because if somebody like George Waterston comes in you'll go to gaol for ten years and also be fined about £15,000!'

'Calm down my dear friend,' said Donald, impeccably smooth as always, but totally missing the point. 'Two of my men brought them off the Island yesterday. I can prove it.' But it was all right. Despite the fact he had swiped every last egg, the roseate terns laid again and the colony survived.

# 9. | Pigeons

If Noah was the first person to have used the exceptional homing instincts of a pigeon to his own ends, he has a lot to answer for. In the last War homing pigeons were so important as message bearers at time of radio silence from the Atlantic convoys, that their greatest natural enemy the peregrine falcon, although even then a rare and much valued bird, was systematically shot and poisoned by our panicky War Department and is now, despite all our efforts to save it, in danger of becoming extinct in this country. Long ago message-bearing homers gave rise to the sport of racing pigeons, in which in Europe more money is said to pass hands each year than in horse racing. In Britain even the Queen has her royal loft and as a participatory sport it is second only to angling.

My friend Henry Trotter took it up when he retired from his

Mastership. He spent a fortune on a luxury loft and filled it with birds of the most immaculate pedigree. I used to see him careering about the county in his landrover training them for the long-distance races ahead.

'Just bought one for £600. Might let him out soon,' he would say.

'You're mad,' I would tell him. 'It will hardly find its way back the ten miles from Coldstream let alone from Rouen or Bordeaux!'

One Saturday he asked me over to await the return of his current favourite from its first competition. The birds had been released somewhere in England that morning and after lunch we retired to the loft with a decanter of port to welcome what Henry was sure would be the winner. We finished the port and still there was no sign of the bird. I left him pacing up and down his yard and arrived back at my house three miles distant to find the bird on my window-sill.

'Your bird's here!' I announced over the telephone.

'Eat it!' he barked slamming down his receiver.

A racer that fails to find its loft even once is a write-off. I did not eat it but let it disseminate its long pedigree among the steading pigeons at the farm.

Pigeon racing is a heart-breaking sport. Henry once had to shoot his best bird when it arrived back in spectacular time because it refused to come into the loft to let him stop the clock. And once my brother Alec, despite all our shouts that the birds coming over him were not the golden plover he thought they were, brought off a brilliant right and left at racers during a grouse drive at Douglas. He also happened to be the local M.P. and it transpired that one of these precious ringed birds belonged to one of his mining constituents who, unluckily for Alec, happened to be out that day as a beater. Alec thought it would cost him a fiver at the outside, but he found himself anted up to the tune of £15. 'Yon was the best bird I ever bred,' said the self-termed owner with a wink as he pocketed the cash.

The rock dove is the ancestor of both these pampered racing pigeons and the grubby ferals which swarm the cities of the world: the racer, refined by generations of breeding, as close as you could get to a pedigree rock; the feral a mongrel, its few traces of original stock eradicated by hundreds of years of promiscuity. The true rock dove now only exists in the wild state on the most isolated sea cliffs of the northwest coasts of Scotland and Ireland. Doves seen in sea caves elsewhere will be flocks of ferals that have reverted to a semi-wild state.

The domestication of pigeons literally dates 'from the Flood', but in comparatively recent times the introduction of the dovecot undoubtedly played its part in harbouring mixed pigeon colonies. As most pigeons will nest all the year round given favourable circumstances, dovecots provided an unfailing supply of food which must have been a godsend in the frugal winters and sieges of medieval times. Ferals today are ubiquitous and a perfect pest if you are trying to preserve a particular strain of decorative dove like a fantail or tumbler. Within a few days the local feral males will have gathered like a bunch of tomcats and soon the offspring of your treasured doves will be showing all the tell-tale imperfections of a feral father. It is useless shooting them. They keep so close together that you will probably end up with your fantails dead and the ferals back on the roof. However they are far from being stupid birds. There was a pair in Newcastle which regularly used to take a ship to Kristiansand in Norway. I did not believe this, but the ship's captain assured me that it was true and sure enough as we headed out to sea from Tynemouth these two ferals came aboard. They settled down quite happily for the voyage and then, before we entered port on the other side, took off into the town to consort with their Norwegian friends until the ship made its return passage, the two of them following us out to sea as before.

I did a number of cruises to Scandinavia. On one occasion as we finally disembarked the purser kindly handed me a farewell present of a box of slides: 'Here's some birds I think you'll find of interest, Henry,' he said. I banked them with my others and I am afraid had forgotten all about them by the time I got home. Some months later I had to give one of my bird lectures to warm up a vast conference of conservative ladies gathered for a political rally at the Peebles Hydro Hotel. Everything went smoothly until, to my horror and the consternation of the audience, a seductively posed nude model appeared on the screen. I hurried on but it was no good. Another even more erotic siren came up. I had struck the purser's 'birds'! The audience left in indignant droves and were only gathered together again with the greatest difficulty for Alec's climacteric speech to the conference on the following night.

The rock dove, with its preference for cliffs was probably our first pigeon, but as soon as these islands finally emerged from the ice the wood pigeon and the stock dove cannot have been long in following. Like many other species, both birds have been more effected by today's farming methods than by anything else in their history. Wood pigeons feed on fallen fruit berries, beech mast and acorns – I have counted thirty-six large acorns in a crop – curdling this food into a milk and regurgitating it at the nest when they have young to feed. Over the centuries they have also become very dependent on good cropping. The permanent clover pastures, greens, turnips, stooks and spilled corn of pre-combine harvested fields and all the other trimmings of less efficient days were very much to their taste. Now they have to forage wider and farther, their numbers fluctuating in accordance with the food supply.

As usual an albino is an invaluable marker of the movements of the bird in general. The only one I recall at Hirsel arrived each autumn and disappeared the following spring for three consecutive years. But, most surprisingly, despite alerting ornithological clubs we never received one report of its being sighted in the intervening periods.

Wood pigeons are continually on internal migration to fresh food areas. Once at Douglas I discovered large numbers of them at least eight miles from the nearest wood, flighting on to a large lump of salt which had been dumped in the middle of a rough pasture next to the moors as a lick for the cattle. Seasonal abundance of food also makes them predominantly autumn nesters, although unlike most birds they are prepared to do so at any time of the year, even in December snow if food stocks allow it. They are prolific breeders. One pair was reliably reported to me of having raised six broods in nine months from the same nest in a creeper on a house in east Ross-shire.

From the end of October there are huge immigrations of darker coloured wood pigeons from the north, which as children we were brought up to call 'Norwegians'. When I brought the matter up with Miriam Rothschild, an authority on the bird, she told me that there was no evidence of any noticeable migration of pigeons into Britain from Scandinavia or anywhere else, and that so-called 'Norwegian wood pigeon' were home-grown birds moving south from the forests of north-east Scotland. I have similarly found no evidence of wood pigeon being reported in any numbers from the coastal bird stations and have never seen these darker birds on any of my trips to Scandinavia. But, although I cannot support my theory, I still believe they are of a different type to the home-grown bird.

I told her about Eric Linklater, the author, who lived on Orkney and was rung up one day by a friend to come and shoot wood pigeon. Eric had never seen more than the occasional wood pigeon on Orkney in his life and decided the Highland Park whisky was to blame for this interruption, but he went along all the same and, despite both of them being rotten shots, they got fifty-six. The birds were coming in all day off the sea from the direction of Norway. Miriam said they must have been blown off course from the Scottish mainland.

Woodpigeon, like mallard, are wild birds which have domesticated themselves to live in cities, yet no bird is more difficult to approach in open country. They have astonishingly acute hearing and eyesight and are capable of violent changes of direction if surprised in flight. These attributes, combined with their under-estimated excellence as meat and often destructive numbers, have made them a much shot bird. After the war there were even free cartridges issued to control their numbers. Naturally great efforts were made to shoot off most of these at legitimate targets but quite a few of them, not surprisingly, brought down the odd pheasant as well. At Hirsel, pigeon shoots, involving if possible one gun in every wood to keep the birds on the move, used to take place every week throughout the winter with, despite huge bags, very little effect on the numbers of the birds. The poisonous seed-dressings which were used with such abandon later on, could destroy more of them in an afternoon than we probably did in all our shoots put together.

One Good Friday in the late 'fifties there were pigeons dropping dead all over Hirsel and its neighbouring estates. The cause was eventually traced to an innocent farmer who had sown seed barley with double the normal dose of dressing. I took the matter up politically and eventually received an assurance from the Secretary of State for Agriculture that he would look into the matter but that in the meantime I should remember that more birds died every year from natural causes than from poison! I often wonder how he would have altered this priceless estimate if two or three atom bombs had exploded in the Borders. The situation is publicly said to be better now but the large number of dead birds of all types that I still find each spring makes me have my doubts.

The trouble is that there is no way in which the vague govern-ment pronouncements can be enforced. The instructions on most bags of seed-dressing are as vague as those on a carton of cigarettes. If anyone has been arrested for the improper use of a dressing I have yet to hear of it. Mercury is known to be a bird killer and as a result farmers are urged to use it only for dressing winter wheat, and other crops normally sown in the autumn, when birds will be least likely to crop it because of the abundance of other food. But much winter wheat is sown later, in a hard winter perhaps not till February when birds are voracious, with the obvious reverse effect to the one intended. This is but one example of many. There are no rules, because it is not in a government's interest to have any.

There has always been a craze for pigeon shooting, although it amounted almost to a fever during the free ammunition period after the War. Two brothers who were neighbours of ours, General and Professor Collingwood, were coming to shoot at Hirsel one snowy afternoon and when their aged mother refused to let them borrow her sheets they went to their local church and 'borrowed' some vestments instead! My father was horrified: 'Sacrilege, my dear fellow.' But there was no divine retribution – they both shot over forty. As for a friend of mine in Hampshire, he killed a hundred within fifty yards of his village church, not even letting up for the vicar's sermon.

This magic hundred was always eluding William and once he asked me to find him a field where he could finally achieve it as he was coming north for a few days. I had returned to the army by the time he arrived but it was during the harvest and I had no difficulty in discovering a stubble on which hundreds of wood-pigeons were feeding. I told him where it was and even left instructions as to where he should position his wooden decoys. The day he chose was gloriously hot and everything went to plan. He was out early before the cobwebs were off the fields, the decoys worked like a charm and by early in the afternoon, when at last there was a lull in the flight, he was safely into his eighties. The remainder of the day would doubtless assure him of his hundred, so in happy contemplation of this achievement and no doubt musing on how he could introduce it into the plot of his next play, he decided to take time off for a well-earned lunch and enjoy the sunshine. He finished his sandwiches and about half-a-gallon of beer, fell asleep with his dream in view and woke to find the pigeons back at their feed. Befuddled he drew a bead and then another and then another until, after a few minutes, finding that none of the birds had taken off he tottered out and discovered they were his unhappy decoys. He still has not managed a hundred.

Not all William's attempts at identification were so wayward. In 1946 he was the first person to be officially credited with seeing a turtle dove's nest in Scotland. Turtle doves are summer visitors only and for years they had been extending their breeding range farther and farther north. I was convinced that one day they would arrive at Hirsel, but when they did I was in Norway. William telephoned me the news. They were nesting in a rhododendron bush below the dining-room window, the female was sitting on eggs and could he take a photograph.

'For heaven's sake,' I said. 'It's the only pair ever known to nest in Scotland. Leave it alone.'

'How long do they take to sit on the eggs? She's sitting on two eggs.'

I said I thought it was about twenty-one days.

'Right ol' man. I promise I won't go near them.'

On the twenty-first day precisely he forced his way into the bush armed with his No. 2 Brownie, almost physically assaulting the bird in the process, took a photograph which did not come out, and was surprised when the turtle doves headed straight off to South Africa without further delay.

Luckily I had a second chance. In 1953 I heard one calling and we soon discovered the nest, this time in a currant bush next to the path between the drive and the stables. If we could protect this bird from any interference we should after all have the first officially confirmed case of the turtle dove hatching young north of the Border. For the birds' sake we hushed the thing up but somehow, as always seems to happen, news of its presence soon began circulating in ornithological circles. 'Now look here,' George Waterston telephoned me from Edinburgh, 'you've got all these experts coming down and they want to see this turtle dove you've got.'

'Oh really? First I've heard of it,' but it was no good.

'It's a risk, but you've got to show them it. Many of them'll want to verify it and anyway it'll be one of the sightings of their lives.'

'All right,' I agreed reluctantly.

Hirsel tours traditionally start from the stables, so in the days following George's command my niece Caroline and I gradually familiarised the unhappy female with the condition of having 180 ornithologists filing past on a gravel path. Every day at 11 o'clock, the hour at which the tour would start, we set out from the stables singing, talking, scuffing the stones and generally behaving like lunatics and walked past the turtle dove's bush at diminishing distances until, on the day before the party's arrival, we had conditioned the birds to put up with all this noise from a range of about six feet, which was close enough to give a good view of the sitting female and also enabled us to walk on the silence of the grass verge. The female had looked increasingly perplexed but stayed put. On the day I told everyone to keep moving as they walked past and not, on any account, to look directly at the bird in case they fatally caught its eye. To supervise this I stood with a walking-stick pointed at the nest so that by looking down it they could instantly locate the bird and move on in a single movement. Everything went like clockwork until the arrival of the very last person, an old lady, who grabbed the end of my stick and was bashing about in the leaves for a better view before I realised what was happening. Of course the bird was off in an instant. It returned to our relief, but eventually failed to raise the brood because of a later raid by jackdaws when the squabs were only a week old. Since then they have returned quite regularly to Hirsel and successfully raised young there and elsewhere in Scotland.

## 10. | Owls

One still September evening waiting for duck in a hide of oat stooks, I was watching a barn owl quartering the field in front of me: noiseless as a moth in the silence, luminously following the lines of the stooks to the distant fence before quartering back again. I saw it pounce twice. It was a hopeless night for duck, far too quiet, but peaceful. Watching the owl whiled away the time. It grew darker. I strained to hear the whisper of mallard wings and suddenly felt a waft of air on the back of my neck, the gentlest of evening breezes, and turning found myself confronting the ghostly face of the barn owl. It had obviously come to see if my cap could be eaten. The shock was reciprocal. It moved away as silently as it had arrived.

Of all the owls the barn is the gentlest and most entertaining. As a pet it enjoys nothing better than to sit on your lap with its eyes closed being stroked and tickled like a cat, even purring to show its pleasure. The difficulties of bringing them up however should not be underestimated. For six weeks they look like snakes, and throughout have to be fed small pieces of meat wrapped in the roughage of feathers or fur, but eventually you will have as beautiful and affectionate a bird as you could imagine. They are also quite capable of supporting themselves when reintroduced into the wild. I have reared several over the years and I am convinced that the last one is still about, because a barn owl flys past peering at the windows some afternoons and can be seen generally hanging around the garden. Tawnies also make very charming pets as chicks because of their fluff ball appearance. The parents will not feed them if they fall out of the nest so if you find one on the ground you are saving its life by bringing it home.

The most memorable owl I have had in my care belonged to one of my cousins. She telephoned me with the news that she had found a lovely specimen of a tawny by the side of a burn outside Haddington. Tawnies often go into a moribund state like this in cold weather, so despite her insistence that it was absolutely stone-cold dead in front of her on the kitchen table I suggested she warmed it up by laying it by the fire, and call me back. Half-an-hour later she was on the line in a state of great excitement to say that the owl was still on its side but had woken up and laid an egg. I never heard what happened to the egg but the owl thrived and she doted on it. Unfortunately she also had a husband who was an acting admiral and every now and then she had to go and look after him as well. One of these trips to Malta was threatening and she began to pester me for ideas as to what could be done with the owl in her absence. I was on army duty close by in Edinburgh, but there was no question of my being able to look after the bird because I was living in the New Club, the most exclusive male preserve in Scotland and absolutely bristling with admirals, generals, porters and starched housemaids. I must have told my cousin this a hundred times, but one night I was summoned from the bar to meet what the hall-porter po-facedly announced as 'a visitor', who had arrived by

taxi, and inevitably turned out to be my cousin's owl. She had
sent it from Haddington and done a bunk. From then on my life
was a nightmare of stealth and deceit. I smuggled the bird
everywhere as unconcernedly as possible, but the alteration in my
behaviour soon began to be commented on by the members.

'I know there's rationing old boy,' a General remarked at
dinner one night as I was tipping some of the owl's favourite
sardines off my plate and into an envelope, 'but hoarding
sardines seems to be taking things a bit far.'

'I've been watching him,' said another. 'Does it quite often.
Most extraordinary.'

'May have to go on duty later,' I explained without much
conviction.

At night the owl sat on the bed-rail turning its head through
360° and occasionally, to my dismay, answering the calls of a

neighbouring bird in Princes Street Gardens. By day she accompanied me to my office in a box. She always liked to know where she was and had everyone swooning away when she poked her head out on the trams or from the luggage-racks of railway carriages. But one night I was summoned from my room by an urgent telephone call and left the door open. When I got back the owl had gone. I rushed into the passage and as I did so heard an awful scream from the landing followed by a crash enough to shake the foundations. I arrived to find the bird sitting nervously at the head of the bannisters with a rather intoxicated full Colonel lying on the floor. His bald head was bleeding.

'God Henry,' he gasped. 'I've been attacked by a monster.'

'Steady on,' I said. 'I know exactly how you feel. It often happens to me when I drink port.'

'Thing like a vulture,' he muttered confusedly as I helped him to his feet. Next day the Secretary took me aside:

'The peculiarity of your bedroom habits has been a cause of wonder to the staff for some time,' he said gravely. 'Now Colonel Sprott is convinced that the upstairs passage is haunted by a vulture. At an emergency meeting of the Club Committee this morning it was unanimously agreed that either you or your vulture must leave forthwith – preferably both.'

Happily for the owl it was then that my cousin returned. I was very sad. It had been a trusting character of great charm, entirely incapable of looking after itself. I warned my cousin of this but alas on another flying visit she forgot to leave the poor bird enough food, and although she was only away five days it had starved to death by the time she returned. This is always the risk in taking on any wild thing: so often they become completely dependent. Meanwhile the Colonel wandered the New Club spreading the news that I had been harbouring vultures in my bedroom.

Tawnies have always suffered persecution from gamekeepers and the scolding of other birds, both quite unmerited. In Hertfordshire I was once shown a little owl's nest which contained the remains of at least thirty pheasant and partridge chicks, but despite the conviction of numerous keepers these rogue birds of prey are always the exception. Being night hunters owls rarely see chicks in any case. As for songbirds, I am convinced they scold owls as a reaction to the shock of discovering that what they took to be a branch suddenly opened an eye. Songbirds scold stoats and snakes in just the same way but for better reason.

The tawny's 'towit-towoo' is such a classic that I was particularly keen to make the best possible recording of it, and one April I persuaded Melville Dinwiddie, Controller of the B.B.C. in Scotland, to put all his sound equipment at our disposal for this purpose. We had half-a-dozen mikes out in Dundock but either because they heard our apparatus working or because the weather was cold and wet, the owls were struck dumb. After two or three days Dinwiddie became very agitated because he was shortly going to need the outside broadcast unit for an important football match in Glasgow. He telephoned more and more dementedly until at the end of the week he appeared at Hirsel in person.

'Either you've all been down at the pub every night or this is the only place in Britain where there are no owls, but whatever the reason there's going to be an owl tonight. That equipment was due back three days ago. It's ridiculous.'

'We may be lucky, but honestly it's been the weather. You wait and see,' I said, looking at the leaden skies.

William was home at the time and had shown a close interest in the proceedings but on the evening of Dinwiddie's visit he disappeared after dinner. I did not blame him. I wished I could have done the same myself. The rest of us trooped down in the dripping darkness to the control van in the wood.

'Not a good night,' I said as our first mikes drew a blank.

'Nonsense,' replied Dinwiddie. 'Let me run this show. Give me No. 5.' He switched on to the fifth microphone a hundred yards away in the bushes from where we sat and to our amazement the most wonderful owl call we had ever heard came smoothly down the line. You could literally hear its intakes of breath. Dinwiddie was triumphant. 'Nothing wrong with your fieldwork, Henry, I'll give you that. You must just remember to turn the mike on next time that's all.' Back at the house William reappeared to ask how things had gone. 'Perfect,' I said. 'Literally perfect.' And it was true. The recording was an instant success. It became the standard for any B.B.C. nature programme on owls and soon found, and still finds, its way into plays and serials. Years later William casually brought up the subject.

'Do you remember old Dinwiddie and the owl?' he asked.

'Of course I do.' I still winced at the thought of it.

'I'm afraid it was me old man.'

And immediately I remembered how suspiciously absent he had been on the night.

'You twister!' I exclaimed. But it was too late to do anything about it, so for years whenever B.B.C. Drama sent Juliet out on her balcony or Frankenstein up to his laboratory they would be accompanied, for those few of us in the know, by the distant sound of William hooting.

In 1966 there was an eagle owl seen in Berwickshire: magnificent birds, for which a rabbit is a mere starter. They devour pigeons, hares, even young roedeer. The plumage is like an eagle's and their brilliant orange eyes are worthy of a tiger. This sighting was first made by a young girl who was working as a chemist's assistant in Coldstream. She used to bicycle two miles into the town every morning and one day as she unlatched the gate at home she saw a huge bird on the gate-post, the size of a turkey. She screamed and ran for her life. The laird of the property telephoned me later and I went over to make an inspection with him. It transpired that several of the locals had noticed this incredible bird for a week or two. We searched a shelter strip of spruces behind the farm where it had been seen killing a pigeon and found the mangled corpses of ten or more, and next day a huge owl was reported at Hirsel. It then vanished and was not reported again. I never saw it but the descriptions and the state of the dead pigeons left me in no doubt as to what it was. It could have been an escaped bird, but still made an awesome impression. No zoo collection reported the loss of an eagle owl, so it was a pity that we did not notify the experts and have its presence verified.

## 11. | The swift

Of all the birds I have come across in my life the swift is the most fascinating, and I have devoted more time to them than to other species.

Swifts are perhaps our most noticeable bird in summer. Over practically every town and village and group of old buildings throughout the British Isles you will see them wheeling and diving: sometimes at great heights, each bird hunting separately for insects which form its only diet; sometimes in screeching packs almost at ground level, weaving and darting round every available obstacle in exultation at their unrivalled control of flight. It is this domination of the air which makes them so different to all other birds and particularly from swallows and martins with which they often share the sky. But unlike them swifts never perch. They never congregate on telegraph wires or roofs. The size of their feet will not allow it.

## The swift

I first became intrigued by them when I was a schoolboy at Eton. I had a room which overlooked the old fives courts and every evening in the summer, during that pleasant meditative hour or so when boys were confined to their rooms following prayers and before 'lights' at 10 p.m., I would lean on my window-sill and, usually smoking an illegal pipe I am sorry to say ('borrowed' from my father), watch their antics. The open courts, which faced the expanse of a playing field, provided them with an obstacle set in a space capable of testing their aerobatics to the full. The place would be teeming with swifts, screaming in over the grass, playing in and out of the buttressed concrete and in their excitement overshooting the target so wildly that they would be forced to brush past me at my window, leaving a musty aroma on the air which luckily exactly matched my John Cotton No 1 mixture tobacco.

This meditative hour was also the one in which my house-master Mr C. M. Wells did his rounds and sometimes, I think hoping to catch me for a quiet rebuke, his knock on the door would come at a later time than usual.

'Oh Home. Up very late?' Always the same diplomatic finesse.

'No, no sir. Not at all, just watching these lovely swifts. Beautiful the way they circle around screaming.'

'Weally?' No 'r's' could be rolled in the classical purity of his pronunciation. He would come over and join me at the window. He had a very acute sense of smell.

'They have this odd smell sir. Musty.'

'Hm. Yes I see what you mean. Smells wather like tobacco doesn't it.'

'I suppose it does, sir. Never thought of it like that.'

'Now, tell me about swifts.'

So there I would be, discoursing on swifts with this burning pipe stuffed into my pocket; but eventually the old boy would slouch off in his flapping slippers – 'Intwiguing birds, intwiguing' – and I would be left to my observations and the time perhaps for one more smoke before bed. It was on one of these nights that I witnessed the most dramatic of their habits for the first time. When they stopped playing, just on dark, they all circled up screaming, up and up into the sky, fainter and fainter till they disappeared from sight and could no longer be heard. From that moment I decided swifts were the most fascinating and mysterious of all birds, and nothing I have learned since has shaken that boyish conviction.

Swifts do everything in the air because of their inability to perch. Their circling to high altitudes at night is just one example of this. The intriguing mystery I witnessed at Eton had been solved some years before by aircrews on night reconnaissance over the Western Front in the First World War. They reported seeing parties of them as high as 10,000 feet asleep on the wing. And that is how they roost, drifting, bouyed by the up drafts for the few hours of summer darkness sometimes to heights of over three miles above the earth. Not every swift roosts in this way. In the breeding season I have noticed that nesting birds will often creep into their nesting boxes for a two to three hour siesta of an early afternoon. They have to be airborne to survive, which explains why they spend the shortest time of any migrant in this country: being assured of the best of the weather and the maximum amount of sunlight and insects. They are to the skies what the ocean wanderers – albatross, shearwater and petrel – are to the seas, but unlike them the swift cannot rest at will. It can crawl into crevices and on to ledges, it can cling to vertical rough surfaces, but to fly again it must be able to fall free. Its minute feet are too frail to support the weight of its body. A swift on the ground is almost helpless. To fly it must have a height to topple off. In this dependence on the air it would seem to be the most evolved of any bird, the least land based, the most efficient in flight – the most tireless as well as the fastest. It is airborne for most of its life. It feeds in the air, mates in the air, drinks by swooping to water, and gathers nesting materials in the air.

The European swift arrives here in the first days of May from the region of South Africa, south of Johannesburg to the Cape. Mating is heralded by a very sharp and persistent twittering from the female who hovers at a height of about 200 feet, and is then borne down almost to ground level by the male before both break again into separate flight. Wisps of straw and pigeon feathers are gathered from the air. The nest is built in the gaps at the juncture of roof and wall in old buildings and always at a sufficient height to allow the birds to swoop up from below on entry and fall out on departure. In the village of Greenlaw I have seen them nesting as low as ten feet from the ground amid all the business of a garage on a main street, but this is unusual. To make the nest they chew to form saliva and then use this as a lubricant with which to stick the materials together. The result is a tiny shallow cup about the size of a tea-cup saucer which sets as hard as porcelain. In the Far East a very similar nest of another variety of swift, melted down, provides the main ingredient of birds nest soup.

The nesting of swifts is lengthy and arduous. From May till mid-July the parent birds are uniquely subject to the demands of the young, because these cannot leave the nest until they are able to fly. This usually takes six weeks from the time of hatching so two broods are out of the question, although cold weather can often delay nesting and cause late clutches. There are normally two to three eggs, never more. Through studying swifts in boxes I soon realised how subject they are to weather and how extraordinary the depths of their resources in combating its ill effects. The first thing I noticed was that if the temperature dropped to near freezing, as it can do in the North in May, all the adult birds would disappear, sometimes for as much as four days. Research has shown that these journeys occur when local insect food becomes scarce. Swifts in this predicament will travel unimaginable distances in search of warmer weather. Radar has revealed that a Border bird for instance thinks nothing of making a round trip as far as the Baltic in a single day to gather flies, and since they are capable of speeds of up to 100 mph this may not be the limit of their daily range. The other features of their behaviour during these cold spells were even more puzzling, and took me longer to solve.

Walking at the foot of the wall to which the boxes were nailed I sometimes noticed broken swift eggs on the gravel. At first I assumed this was the result of invading house sparrows or of the fights between the swifts themselves or even of wind or carelessness. But these falls were so persistent at certain times that I eventually began to keep a closer watch. Possibly some change of barometric pressure warns them of an impending insect shortage, because it is often just in advance of these times that the parent birds themselves clear the nests of eggs. Young birds produced a different problem. I came across apparently dead and abandoned young lying in the boxes, motionless and stone cold. I was to discover that this too was caused by insect shortages. The birds were not dead but in suspended animation in the expectation of the return of their parents from one of those lengthy food forays. As with the eggs, when I actually watched a female perform the manoeuvre of tipping them overboard, I happened to be there when a parent bird returned with the fruits of its wanderings: a congealed ball of flies about the size of a marble swelling its throat. In half-an-hour it had warmed and cajoled its young into a state of full consciousness. The juveniles then wait for their flight feathers to grow. The parent birds sense when this time has come. They feed the young much less and come in later to roost. For two days the young are as restless as mice and then on the third morning the nest will be empty. The parents usually delay their departure for a few days longer. I have never seen a young swift in flight. It seems that from the moment they fall from their nests they are outward bound for Africa and south of the Equator.

None of these insights would have been possible were not swifts, because of their aerial lives, the birds most impervious to human interference. My observations were mostly done by lifting the lids of the boxes, and I was constantly amazed by their trusting behaviour. Despite the irritation of my surveillance there was not a single case of desertion.

Contrary to their black appearance in the air swifts are mouse coloured birds, but just as beautiful in detail in the hand as on the wing. Their breeding plumage refracts green and purple and both sexes have a patch of white feathers on the throat. This patch is I think more pronounced in the male bird, whose head is generally less grey than the female's, though the difference is so marginal that for general purposes it can be said that the sexes are indistinguishable. Swifts are about six-and-a-half inches long. The beak is typical of an insect feeder: small for pinching, but capable of a gape almost as wide as a nightjar's. The eye is sinister and reptilian, socketed under hooded eyebrows as comparatively prominent as a peregrine's. These hoods protect the eye from the friction of the wind and permit clear vision despite the enormous speeds that have to be withstood. The new born young look decidedly reptilian. When the bird is in repose the wing tips cross each other and stick out to either side of the tail.

About two summers after my initial interest in the birds at Eton I was forced to spend one summer term at home to convalesce after a severe attack of measles. It was thought that my heart had been strained, so when the weather permitted I was parked outside in a deckchair in the lee of the East wing at Hirsel to pass the days as quietly as possible in a state of placid ease. At least, that is what it would have been without the swifts. Most of them I knew, nested in the spires of the two churches in Coldstream nearby but soon I realised that there was one fiercely contested nesting site on the East wing itself. This was a crevice in the stone just under one of the gutters. That summer, from my deckchair, I was privileged to see the entire performance: the desperate struggles of over fifty pairs trying to take possession of the site on arrival (David Lack in his classic study of the bird *Swifts in a Tower* describes two swifts being locked in combat on the floor of a site for over five hours); the subsequent occupancy of the triumphant pair; the way in which the disappointed Coldstream birds returned every evening to visit their friends and play and feed around the house. Obviously Hirsel was a favourite place, but it took a long time for the penny to drop. In fact not until after the War. One day I remembered this old natural site and decided to see if it was still in use. It was, and at last I thought of duplicating it to form a nesting colony. I thought briefly of hacking holes under the gutters, but after a while I quietened down and began to think of how to devise equivalent spaces in the form of nesting boxes. So I had some made and hung them under the windows in a window-box position in order that the lids could be lifted with ease for inspection. My father thought I was raving mad. 'You'll never persuade a swift to nest in a nesting-box. Nobody's ever done it and nobody ever will,' he said. But he was a patient man and admitted that it was preferable to hacking the house to bits.

After one or two experiments I designed a type of box which proved successful. The first were too small and allowed the entry of house sparrows, but the final product has not failed in over twenty years. They are very simple and hung just below the windowsill, so that the swifts can leave and enter with a clear flight. It is essential to have the flap projecting over the hole to prevent sparrows from taking over. (See diagram on p. 123 and plate 8.) These were successful as the following extracts from my diary of 1953 show:

June   1:  Pair of swifts in and out of one of my boxes by the nursery window. One spent several periods of 10–20 minutes inside the box but there is no sign of building. . . .
June   6:  Swifts in and out of box but still no sign of nest. . . .
June  14:  Swifts spent long time in the box. A small nest cup in the centre but no egg. Both birds roost inside the box at night.
July 10:  Swifts impossible! There are 2 nests. The females sit as if brooding. The males spend each night in the boxes but no eggs. . . .
July 25:  Both pairs roosting on nests in boxes. No eggs. They left about 7.15 a.m. The nests have slightly increased in size, chiefly built of pigeon and pheasants' feathers. No birds there during daylight hours now.

## The swift

July 31:  Both pairs of swifts roosting in boxes at 11 p.m., tightly
pressed against each other. A little scuffling and squeaking
from both pairs as I watched them. . . .

August 1:  Heavy thunder and rain came on at 6 p.m. Both swifts
came into the box at 7.15 p.m. The other box was empty. . .
And then:

August 8:  11 p.m. One swift in the first box. Second pair of boxes
empty.

So that was that. The sparrows had been thwarted, at least all
but the most ingenious of them. To this day my niece Caroline
has to check the boxes a few days before the swifts arrive, about
May 1, but from that second year sparrows no longer constituted
a threat. In 1954 however I did once again enlarge the boxes. In
the swifts' natural nesting sites it was impossible to see how large
the areas were behind those crannies, but I had a feeling they
might well be spacious enough to afford a lot more movement
than I had first imagined. This increase in size worked like a
charm. In 1954 all ten boxes under the top-floor windows of the
East wing were occupied, the first time as far as I know that
swifts had been artificially induced to nest. These ten boxes have
been used every year since. Naturally I tried to put up more than
this because there were literally a hundred pairs on the waiting list,
but only the top-floor windows seemed high enough for them
and the other side of the house all proved too far to windward.
So the number has always remained ten, but these ten have
nevertheless revealed some astonishing facts.

To keep records was obviously the next step and in 1957, by
which time the colony had become securely established all the
occupants both young and old were ringed for the first time.
This was an extremely delicate task – the minute swift leg takes
the smallest ring available to any bird – so from the first the
operation has been performed by an expert. The ringing event
takes place at the darkening, about 11 p.m. in Berwickshire,
usually on the second Sunday of July. By that hour all the roosting adults will be in, and by that date very few of the early broods
will have flown and very few of the late broods will still be too

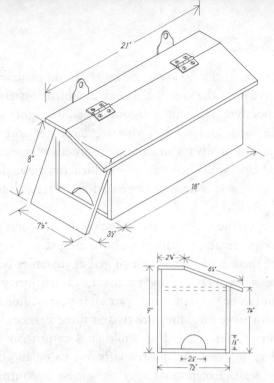

## SWIFT BOXES

1. This design has proved 100% perfect since 1954–55.
2. Preferably made with seasoned wood (but not necessary) to avoid future warping.
3. Hinges must be *strong*.
4. Aspect immaterial. At Hirsel we use East and South faces of the house. We gave up Western face owing to Westerly prevalent winds – often gale force – which shake and even dislodge boxes. Both East and South boxes do equally well.
5. Any aspect above 15 feet suitable particularly in village or urban area.
6. *Always put up at least 3 boxes* close to each other. Remember that swifts are 'social' nesters, and prefer to be in company.
7. Do nothing about the 'old nest'. Leave it for another year. Perhaps a spray of insecticide, when they have gone, may freshen it up.
8. Outside of box can be stained with any dye to conform to surrounding colour of building. *NOT* inside.
9. The 'flap' is absolutely necessary to try and prevent House Sparrows from taking over. Even with it, they will try to, and sometimes succeed in, forcing an entry! Add another 2 inches to the length shown above if you want to make absolutely sure.
10. *All boxes* should be inspected and if necessary cleared of 'squatters' *before May 1* each year.

small to ring. In the darkness the holes are momentarily blocked by an envelope, the lids lifted and the birds gently removed. That manoeuvre successfully accomplished the lights are switched on in the room and we see what we have got and ring where necessary. This is always an exciting moment as one can never be sure what one will discover: an old bird returning for a record number of years; a new unringed adult; a rare clutch of three young.

Since 1957 these checks have disclosed an astonishing 90 per cent average return to Hirsel of birds ringed in previous years. A few of these birds have been ringed as juveniles but as can be imagined with such a slow turnover, the majority of nesting adults tend to be the same birds year after year. Adult swifts probably do not mate until they are two or three years old, so as most of our birds were ringed as adults and return on average for eight years, it seems that most swifts live to be about the age of eleven at least. Exceptional ages cannot be uncommon because two Hirsel birds ringed as breeding adults in 1959 returned for fourteen years. Nor did they remain paired throughout that period. While the male bird, on being rejected by his first mate in 1960, contentedly settled down with another female in the box in which he had first been ringed, the female had two further mates and several different homes before returning to rear two young with her original mate in 1973. If these swifts can be assumed to have reached an age of at least seventeen, and if David Lack is right in supposing that a swift flies a daily average of five hundred miles, then the two Hirsel birds must each have travelled over three million miles in their lives.

Most swifts leave this country by the middle of August. Unlike the perching summer migrants like swallows and warblers, swifts effortlessly fly over the normal hazards of migration like drought, poisons and netting, and this undoubtedly explains their robust numbers. Although the few records which exist suggest that their seven thousand mile migration may take as long as a month, I think that for many of them it may take as little as a few days in favourable conditions. Swifts travel at great heights so that one seldom sees them on migration. Only the most severe weather conditions will halt their passage. The only time I have ever seen European swifts on migration was in North Senegal when one night a violent sandstorm forced a pack of three hundred to cling closely to the mosquito wiring of our rest-house. I was equally disturbed for there were many holes in the mosquito net.

There are many races of swifts in the world, some of which can be confused with our European swift *Apus apus*, except in their breeding areas which for geographical reasons do not usually coincide. The alpine swift *Apus melba*, the largest and most magnificent of the family, is brown on the upper parts and very white below. David Lack in his book 'Swifts in a Tower' relates this delightful anecdote (or fable):

'In the Edwardian heyday the great Lord Rothschild was sitting with his colleague Dr Hartart in a hotel in St Moritz when he rose in excitement exclaiming: "Ach – there's Melba!" The fashionable crowd rose hoping to glimpse the famous singer.

' "Are you sure?" said the Doctor.

' "Yes," said Lord Rothschild, "I recognised her by her white belly!" '

In Africa I became enthralled by the palm swift, which builds its nest underneath the tip of a palm leaf. The whole of their nesting life is therefore carried on upside down, even to the extent of their having to cement their eggs to the inside of the nest cup to prevent them falling out. Considering the whiplash effect of wind on the branches in tropical storms it is amazing the bird has survived at all. The nesting boxes required for the European bird are simple to make and require no upkeep. Presented correctly at sufficient heights on the sheltered side of a building they will be occupied. I have always thought they would be particularly suited to modern tower blocks of flats.

A few years ago when my brother was Prime Minister the Queen and Prince Philip visited Hirsel and Alec asked me if I would entertain Philip for about an hour while he saw the Queen on some confidential state business. It was at the slackest point of the bird season – in early July, and the only thing I could think of that might amuse him were the swifts. 'Oh!' Alec said, 'that's a very good idea.' I took Prince Philip out and showed him the boxes. He was thrilled. In fact I could not drag him away:

'I've got a marvellous idea. Where can I get some?' He asked. Naturally I told him I would get him some. Then one of his staff came running out and said they were behind schedule for the plane he had to catch later that day at Prestwick for South America, so we hurried indoors. 'I've been looking at these marvellous swift boxes of Henry's, marvellous things,' said Prince Philip. 'And I'm getting twenty-five to put on the terrace at Windsor. Ideal place for them.' And then turning to me he said: 'Don't forget will you? Get them ordered straight away.'

'Well, sir,' I said, 'there's no hurry because as you know the birds won't be back till next May.'

'Well get them ordered straight away anyway. Mad on them.'

With which Her Majesty said that the terrace was where they went if they were eating outside, and she wanted the place to be tidy. But Prince Philip did not bat an eyelid. He looked me straight in the face and said:

'Nonsense. That's perfectly all right. Henry tells me they're the only bird that doesn't make messes!'

'Really?' Her Majesty turned to me.

'Yes, Ma'am,' I mumbled, and said something about their being very clean birds, so H.R.H. got his way. Anyway, to me there was no hurry and after about three weeks I telephoned my friend George Waterston in Edinburgh and again emphasising the lack of urgency, told him that Prince Philip wanted twenty-five boxes for Windsor by the following spring.

'I know,' he said. 'You're a bit late in the day old boy. We got that order three weeks ago.'

And believe it or not Prince Philip, despite all the other things on his mind, had sent a signed message to George Waterston from Prestwick, obviously assuming I would forget.

## 12. | Weather and rarities

The destructive effects of weather on birds should never be underestimated. People tend to forget that all birds are as dependent on liquid as food, that a drought can be just as disastrous as a freeze. In the south of England the heath fires of 1976 almost extinguished the few surviving colonies of the dartford warbler, but no single factor in recent years, apart from water pollution, has been more disastrous for European and African birds than the decade of continuing drought on the borders of the southern Sahara. Jack Vincent told me of one occasion when exhausted swallows were settling on any available perch, even on cars and in Durban rooms, at the end of one of these emaciating migrations. Most of our summer migrants have to feed and rest on these journeys – swallows and warblers perhaps every fifty miles or so – and if drought conditions deprive them of food, drink and shade they are doomed when they land.

Winds and storm also take their toll. One morning at Hirsel after a tremendous nightlong gale we came across several Leach's petrels at the foot of the trees they had crashed into as they were carried helplessly eastward off the Atlantic, and on another similar occasion I picked up a little auk that was still alive but too shocked to survive my attempts to feed it on sardine oil in a bath. Other birds adapt to weather. In a hard winter wrens will reinhabit their old nests, sometimes as many as fourteen packing together to keep warm. Long flyers, like ducks and geese, will move to open water. Ptarmigan and snow buntings, like many other ground birds, assume the colours of their habitats for camouflage. But for our resident birds, particularly the woodland varieties, nothing is more deadly than a prolonged freeze.

In Berwickshire the worst winter I can remember began on Boxing Day 1962. Standing on a high ridge my house gets all the weather, but that day when it began to snow I had a feeling it was not going to stop. In twenty-four hours I was sealed in. There are two short private roads into the grounds and both were soon irretrievably blocked by snowploughs as well as snow. The ploughs were quickly buried from sight. To the left of the front door there was a drift of seventeen feet banked against a yew hedge and sloping down into the orchard beyond. My son George used to exercise our donkeys up and down it. One afternoon the doctor got lost visiting me. He had strayed from a narrow ridge of hard snow coming over the fields from the steading in the dark, and on being rescued instead of treating me I had to treat him – with whisky, the only medecine I had available. I did not get out by car till March 7 – sixty-six days later.

The effect of all this on birds is best conveyed by the fact that within four days I was feeding two coveys of partridges, six pheasants, sometimes as many as forty-two woodpigeon and a mass of smaller birds at the foot of my front steps. The larger

9. Swifts: *Above*. An aerial torpedo. (*Aquila*). *Below*. Almost 6-week old young in nest just before departure for South Africa. (*Aquila*).

*10.* Fishing the Weil Stream, Birgham, scene of Admiral Vian's escapade with the corpse. (*Felicity Douglas-Home*).

11. *Above*. With Alex McEwen on the set of STV's 'Alex Awhile'. I contributed interviews and general items about country life, on this occasion shotguns, so we asked Miss Scotland along to cheer us up. Also present Rory McEwen (2nd right), Steve Benbow (right)
*Below*. Roy Rogers on a visit to publicise newest *Trigger* film. Scottish Command entertained him slightly.

12. *Above*. Recording willow warbler by the lake at Hirsel. They have the most melodious song of all: a quiet phrase of utter beauty luckily repeated every 20 seconds through the day from April until September. (*Felicity Douglas-Home*). *Below left*. Recording wood warblers (Brian Johnston luckily in background). Heavy microphone compared with nowadays (in use 1930–1955). *Below right*. Willow warblers: until the young are hatched such ground nests are almost impossible to find. George succeeded in photographing both adults at the site, which is rare. The female has just fed their brood while the male waits its turn. (*George Douglas-Home*).

13. *Above.* Whooper swans taking off in the Borders. (*Felicity Douglas-Home*).
*Left.* This Mute swan had already lost one nest in a flood of Tweed, but, as with many other waterside nesters, its second attempt was built with equal lack of foresight. The eggs, however, hatched successfully.

*14.* As a schoolboy at Eton, George took a series of photographs of a reed warbler and a young cuckoo. Here the monstrous parasite overflows the tiny nest, having long since destroyed the rightful brood, but its little foster-parents continue to adore it.

15. *Above.* With my Indian hill mynah 'Gluck'. Gluck lived for 14 years and died in 1976. It was the only bird I have known actually to have developed a sense of humour. My friends taught it a scurrilous vocabulary which it used with perfect timing at the most inopportune moments. (*Camera Press*). *Left.* Peregrine with Hume's bar-tailed pheasant (*Symaticus Humiae Humiae*), resident of Manipur and North Burma. The species must have been named after one of his ancestors but which of them I do not know. (*Felicity Douglas-Home*).

*16.* With a Barbary dove in the aviary. (*Camera Press*).

birds, normally so wild, did not move when they were watched from the window. But the true damage was not revealed till the spring. At Hirsel all the old tree crevices and nesting-boxes had corpses in them. It took three years for treecreepers and gold-crests to breed again and ten years of mild winter weather to restore the tits and song thrushes to their old numbers. The green woodpecker has still not recovered. The few dippers that survived, being early river nesters, were drowned in the floods when the snow melted. But throughout Britain the bird that suffered most was the kingfisher.

In Scotland kingfishers still remain a rarity. The best chance of seeing one is in the breeding season when their activities are governed by the routine of feeding the young. Fishermen are more likely to spy them than other people, and some absent-minded anglers have been alerted from a doze by a sudden weight on their rod and the sight of the gorgeous little bird perched at its tip. But it is very shy and will be off in a flash as soon as it knows what it has done, leaving the fisherman to return to his lethargy and his beer.

My most serious thoughts about all birds have always been refreshed by fables connected with them from the distant days of memory or invention. They parallel many of our human assumptions of faith. When Noah was becoming worried about his incompetence in navigational skills he asked the kingfisher (then a drab bird like the dipper) to take off from his carrier and find land. The bird returned some hours later – despite its short wings – clad in the most beautiful plumage.

'Have you found landfall?'

'No, sorry, Admiral, I flew up into the blue sky as high as my wings could take me. The sun began to go down with a lovely red glow and I had to return to the Ark before night.'

As he descended the blue tint of the heavens remained on his back and the glow of the sunset placed its tribute on his breast. But – if you place a feather from the back of a kingfisher in any treasured place the blue will vanish as swiftly as daylight dies.

Apart from the kingfisher I suppose the most exotic of the birds that you could see in a British summer are those great rarities this far north: the golden oriole, the bee-eater, the roller and the hoopoe. All of them, except the female orioles which are closest in appearance to the female blackbird, are beautifully plumaged and are therefore certain to attract attention.

One of my neighbours saw a golden oriole when he was driving to a County Council meeting one morning. He has been a countryman all his life, so he was naturally very over-excited by this rarity. He drove like Fangio to the meeting, having delayed to watch the bird, burst in on his fellow members and breathlessly announced the earth-shattering news. 'Quick! Adjourn the meeting! There's a golden oriole!'

'Golden oriole!' They echoed with one voice, and within seconds were all pursuing my friend in a fleet of cars back to the scene of his discovery. Eventually he pulled up on some deserted stretch of road. 'Isn't it beautiful,' he sighed with great self-satisfaction.

'Isn't what beautiful?' queried one of the party.

'The golden oriole!'

'What golden oriole?'

'On the telegraph wire!' And there, on the telegraph wire, sat a cock yellowhammer.

Male orioles are often much more understandably confused with the yellow rumped green woodpecker. Secretive birds, you catch sight of them in flashes, if ever, as they flicker through the woods or across their favourite orchards. In 1976 a pair nested near Alnwick in Northumberland, thirty miles southeast of Hirsel and William swears he saw one once in Dundock.

I personally have only seen golden orioles in France. Before the War I stayed several times with P. G. Wodehouse in his villa at Le Touquet, which was a great place for them. In the evenings P.G. would emerge for a drink on the verandah and the orioles would come down for their evening meal in the shadows at the edge of the lawn. P.G. was extremely ignorant about birds but mad on cats. By day he was just as invisible as an oriole himself but at night he sallied forth to gamble in the town. And when the football season came round he would go off in the afternoons to watch schoolboy football matches. He found them far more entertaining than the more exalted professional kinds.

The roller I have seen in Berwickshire. The postman telephoned me in a great state. Every night when he went to the pub his friends accused him of having D.T.s because of his stories of the pink and blue pigeon he was seeing every morning on his round. I went over immediately to the field he described and there, following a hay-reaper as close as a black-headed gull keeps to a plough, was this lovely bird picking up grubs and insects and then returning to a telephone wire. On the next circuit of the field I stopped the tractor-driver and asked if he had noticed it: oh yes, he said, it had followed him round one field already. It was some kind of pigeon. Somebody must have lost it. I summoned the experts from Edinburgh and they had wonderful views of this amazingly tame specimen. A few weeks after it disappeared a roller was found dead on a golf green at Gleneagles. I believe it was the same bird; whether it was or not it is now in the Perth Museum.

The hoopoe is perhaps the most sensational of all these colourful vagrants, with the black and white dazzle of its round wings, but its most elegant feature is the superb crest. How it received it has endeared me to the hoopoes ever since I learned of this fable many years ago. There are some fascinating legends of birds, none more so than those surrounding that man of all men, King Solomon. Of course variations abound but close examination will reveal that they are often remarkably accurate as ornithology. Jerusalem lies in the path of the summer migration of the hoopoe from Africa into the Balkans and Europe. The story of how it got its crest and how it was subsequently responsible for the momentous meeting between Solomon and the Queen of Sheba bears witness to the fact of this unchanging migration.

On one of his desert campaigns – this was before he settled

down to build his Temple – Solomon for all his wisdom found himself in desperate straits. His staff had let him down by running out of water or ouzo or whatever he liked drinking, there was no shade and while everyone was away on their searches Solomon sat alone and in despair. Suddenly a congregation of hoopoes appeared and shielded him from the sun with their wings.

'We thought we'd come and help you Your Highness,' said the leader of the hoopoes. And there they stayed till the king was rescued.

'Thank you,' replied Solomon. 'Since you have saved my life I am conferring the crest of my favourite bird on you.'

Every year Solomon had a parade of birds and in the year following the gift of his crest the hoopoe failed to attend.

'Where's that bloody hoopoe?' Solomon stormed at his A.D.C. 'I've given him my crest, he's my favourite bird and he is not present on parade. Tell him unless he reports tomorrow he will be executed with all the other hoopoes. They will be extinct.'

'But the hoopoe's your favourite bird, sir,' said the anguished A.D.C.

'I know. I adore the hoopoe but he knows I value these annual parades and he hasn't taken the trouble to turn up. The fellow's in disgrace.'

About three days later the A.D.C. brought in a very be-draggled hoopoe – utterly miserable, starving and uncrested. Solomon said quietly: 'Now look here my dear bird. You know you're my favourite bird. I honoured you with this crest. But unless you've got a very good excuse you've had it. I mean there will never be a hoopoe in the world again!'

'I know Your Majesty, I'm terribly sorry,' replied the bird, but it's the weight I had to carry. I couldn't get back in time.'

'What *do* you mean!'

'Well Your Majesty, when I left you last year you wished me farewell. You said: "You're my favourite bird. I don't know where you're going to but good luck till my next parade."

The awful thing was Your Majesty I met the most lovely woman.'

'A lovely woman . . .,' mused the king.

'After about three days journey I landed in this place and there was the most beautiful woman I've ever seen. After your own heart, sir.'

'Nonsense. I've got a thousand different women.'

'Ah – very different. I spent a long time with her and ate a lot of worms on her lawn but eventually the final day arrived: "I'll have to go back to the King," I told her. "This wonderful man who's given me my crest. He's rather unreliable but he says I'm his favourite bird so I've got to get back for his parade." She sighed: "All right my dear but wait a moment." And she wrote a message on a strip of parchment: "Your bird tells me you are the most wonderful man in the world. Why not come back next year with him?" She wrapped this piece of parchment round my leg and secured it with this golden ring which is so heavy that it pushed me off course and that's why I am late.'

Solomon took the note. 'All right,' he said. 'I still think you're lying but I'll give you another chance. I will send a signal by you back to this woman.

By the way, you haven't described her loveliness.' The hoopoe ardently obliged and after a few weeks when the bird had recovered and grown a new crest Solomon recalled it to his presence.

'Now look here my dear bird,' he said. 'I still think you're lying but here is my message to this lady of yours which I will read to you in case you get lost or robbed on the way: "Solomon does not go to a woman however attractive she is. She comes to him".'

So the little hoopoe went fluttering back to Ethiopia to his lady, the Queen of Sheba, with Solomon's message. And that was how Sheba came to make her visit and why her retinue was headed by a hoopoe. It should also be remembered that this is the first record of a bird being ringed in the history of ornithology.

Occasional hoopoes can go a long distance off their normal course. Shortly after the War I was doing a fortnightly broadcast on nature and had talked about the hoopoe. A few days later I received a letter from a boy in Tiree saying he had found one exhausted on the beach and had been feeding it for a fortnight on soaked oatmeal and bread. I was still in the army and with the kind co-operation of the R.A.F. who called it a 'training flight' the bird was flown to Edinburgh and delivered to the zoo. Unluckily it was so weak after a diet to which it was not accustomed that it died very soon. I imagine it is the only time Solomon's favourite bird had the privilege of such modern, efficient and perhaps slightly unauthorised transport. However we tried, and the Queen of Sheba was not in the R.A.F.

New information of birds for the dedicated naturalist can be just as exciting a discovery as seeing a rarity in the wild. Patrick Chalmers sums it up well in the introduction to his book *Birds Ashore and Aforeshore* of 1935 (also a Collins publication).

'And I found, moreover, that this seeking for material was as exciting as the discovery (did ever I make it) of a new species. When, for instance, I found the legend of the Sea-Pie* and the songsters, when I found the true tale of the inventive Mr Goddard and the Royston Crow† (both of which I retail in their proper places), I was as uplifted as if I had found a colony of Great Auks.'

* In Mr Alexander Moniepenie's 'Birds of Angus and Mearns', printed by Messrs. Black, of Brechin, in 1834.

† In Mr J. Penruddock's 'Tantivy Times' (Ackerman, 1841).

The great bird book collector and factual archivist Hugh Gladstone was still alive at this time, and he was astonished to read the above passage because he had never in all his researches come across Moniepenie and Penruddock. He wrote to his friend Chalmers immediately for details but only received evasive replies: 'I did so much research I simply cannot remember how I came by the works of the authors you mention, but rest assured I shall let you know directly my memory reasserts itself,' and so on. Gladstone dementedly searched the world for the works of the two little known authors and then one day Chalmers, on a visit to Scotland for a lecture, answered his earnest invitations and broke his journey to visit the old boy at Dumfries. No information was forthcoming but a few days later Gladstone received a letter which read something like this:

'My dear Hugh,
    Thank you for my excellent lunch. I feel rather a cad, but I think I will now have to confess that Mr Moniepenie and Mr Penruddock were entirely a figment of the imagination of
                            yours truly,

                    Patrick Chalmers.'

Gladstone felt he had publicly to expose Chalmers to put any other collectors out of their misery who might be at their wits' end looking for the two fictitious authors. I had quite a correspondence with him on the subject and in the end he published Chalmers' admission in a specialist journal, 'The Ibis', with a brief explanation of the circumstances.

    But there was a sequel. I mentioned the incident to the late Duke of Gloucester, who had a bird library second only to Gladstone, and he was most amused and asked for the correspondence. As soon as he received it he contacted his two leading book experts and told them to get him copies of Moniepenie and Penruddock immediately. 'Keep them up to the mark. Keep them up to the mark,' he said when I remonstrated with him, and he derived great amusement from their subsequent reports: a Moniepenie came up for auction at Manchester but went for £100 over the Duke's reserve; a Penruddock at Aberdeen was withdrawn from auction at the last minute, after the Duke had telegraphed to say he would buy it regardless of cost. Eventually, at the end of six months, he sent them each a copy of the relevant 'Ibis'.

## 13. | Migrants

One of the nicest letters I have ever had came from a little girl who had listened to a talk I had given on the cuckoo. 'How is it,' she asked, 'that the cuckoo who has never seen its parents can grow up to say "cuckoo-cuckoo"? If the stork dropped a British baby in China it wouldn't grow up speaking English, would it?' An unanswerable question.

The old cuckoos leave Britain without ever having seen their nestlings, several weeks before these are even fledged, and yet, completely alone, with no knowledge of its own origin and identity, the young cuckoo will find its way to the bird's traditional wintering grounds in central Africa.

Migration is the great mystery of birds. The little arctic tern annually journeys to Antarctica before returning to its northern breeding colonies, in some cases a global round trip of 20,000 miles, the greatest migratory distance covered by any bird. One ringed on the Farne Isles was shown to have completed this odyssey twenty-seven times, an unimaginable feat. Endless research has been done on the homing instincts of racing pigeons but the mystery of such navigation remains as unfathomable as ever. Why do birds migrate and how do they succeed in finding their way so unerringly?

One March morning I was sitting with Jack Vincent in a garden eighty miles inland from Durban. It was ninety degrees in the shade and the trees and bushes were full of the voices of South African birds about which I was trying to learn. Suddenly I felt I was dreaming (as indeed I could have been with the large cane spirit I was sipping). I looked at Jack who smiled: 'Yes. It's all right. That bird may be in the Borders before you' – a willow warbler in full song, seven thousand miles from its possible breeding ground. In three weeks I would be home myself. The first African birds would be arriving at Dundock. Would this same willow warbler be singing there? It is a romance that has been going on for a hundred million years.

The mass of our small migrants are southern birds travelling over land for most of their journey. The little snow bunting migrates south to Britain from Iceland and Greenland, which for a land bird must be the most perilous natural journey of all, carried out as it is almost entirely over the sea. One autumn I discovered an exhausted party of them sheltering in and about the deserted crofts of St Kilda. Later when we had set sail two more came on deck, birds which but for our perch would never have survived the few remaining miles. Most are borne home on the Gulf Stream's prevailing south-westerlies, but if they meet easterlies in the autumn the losses must be appalling. Any perch in such conditions will do, which is what makes the Faeroes, first landfall to the east of Iceland, such a vital link in the migratory chain. The oil platforms on the North Sea will now provide others, just as the old lighthouses did.

In the spring and autumn such places will account for the great proportion of our extreme rarities, but they will also disclose other birds almost as improbable at sea as butterflies: birds that are apparently capable of only fifty yards on land – quail, jack-snipe, leg dangling rails – the darting kingfisher, robins, even goldcrests, the smallest of all European birds, legendarily supposed to migrate by riding on the backs of short-eared owls. Part or all of our population of these migrates every year. And yet you will never see such apparently robust flyers as the larger gamebirds – blackgame, for instance – or, so far as we know, the wood pigeon. Gulls too are lesser sea travellers than you might suppose. Their range usually little more than fifty miles in any given direction from where they are resident, so that the bird that follows your ship through the Mediterranean or the North Sea will in fact be changing all the time as your ship passes from one territory to the next. Coots are no less punctilious. In Africa there is a coot identical in every way to the European bird except that it has red blobs on its forehead above the white cone. The European coot travels throughout the north Mediterranean area into Asia and China, while the African coot dominates the southern shore, yet only very rarely will either bird cross the comparatively narrow divide of the sea.

Many birds return to exactly the same place over and over again, sometimes, if the bird is uncommon, at intervals of several generations. The wryneck has never been a frequent visitor to the north and these days, when it is scarce everywhere, a very rare sight in Berwickshire indeed. However, in 1973 one appeared for several days in a garden in the north of the country. Unfortunately I was away at the time but on my return I referred to Muirhead and found that the only wryneck he mentions was seen on July 31, 1887, within twenty miles of where the current sighting had been made, and in 1964 a wryneck was found alive in a greenhouse at Coldingham Nursery Garden just down the road from it. It is as if the memory has been handed down from one generation to the next. The same is true of most birds, resident and otherwise. The same resting places, the same nesting sites will be used annually or, as in the case of the passing wrynecks, at long intervals. In this way it is often possible to determine where a bird would like to be if conditions allowed it. Providing the Hirsel swifts with boxes was one instance, another was when I attracted pied flycatchers to the valley of the Leet.

Pied flycatchers are African birds which pass along the eastern coast of Britain on their way to nest in their preferred breeding grounds farther north, but many of them will stop in this country if they find a suitable site. At Hirsel there was always a pair up the Leet, but despite ideal conditions – running water and banks of venerable beeches, elms and oaks riddled with possible nest holes – no others ever joined them until I caught their eye with some prominently positioned boxes. Pieds take to boxes as enthusiastically as do the tits. In fact that was the problem: we had to bung the entrances until the last week of April, and even then maintain a constant guard, otherwise the whole lot would have been commandeered by great tits. The Forestry Commission had perfected a box which was demonstrably to the liking of pieds so I bought seventy and fixed them to the trunks of the trees along the valley. The first year five pairs broke off their journey to Scandinavia and settled down for the summer. The next there were thirteen and the year after that twenty-seven, every pair raising a brood successfully. Unfortunately I could not be there to supervise the project longer than this and the untended boxes were all smashed by vandals from Coldstream. I have not had the energy or time to try again, but it shows what can be done beneficially to disrupt the migratory patterns of some species which might otherwise pass us by.

Other migrations are less foreseeable. In 1888 and 1908 there were freak visitations of pallas's sandgrouse from the Middle East, which is why most museums have stuffed specimens dating from those years, and other more regular visitors also appear in large numbers from time to time. Nutcrackers, and more frequently, waxwings are two examples.

The nearest I ever came to seeing a nutcracker at Hirsel was when confined to my bed as a child I was visited by my sisters Bridget and Rachel. They had just seen a bird like a pearly, brown jackdaw disappear into a bramble bush, they reported breath-lessly. I asked them to identify it in the bird book I had by my bedside and they instantly chose the nutcracker. 'Go and get it quick!' I ordered. The whole idea of missing it was too frustra-ting. But after an hour they returned rather crestfallen to say that the brambles had stung too much to let them get inside. Hopeless.

'Waxwing years' are more frequent. Once I watched a flock of them strip a catoneaster bush trained against a house right in the middle of Edinburgh's New Town.

Birds also extend their breeding range so dramatically that it can amount to a migration. The collared dove and the fulmar are the most obvious species to have done this in my life, but at Hirsel there has been no more notable local invasion than that of the green woodpecker, which appeared in the Borders for the first time after the War. Its loud piping was soon a feature of the Berwickshire spring, but the winter of 1962 killed it in such numbers that it is only now beginning to recolonize.

On the whole, however, I have been amazed at the consistency of the migrational patterns of most of the birds I have remarked upon in the record book my father gave me sixty years ago. The numbers of many of the species may have declined but the dates of their arrival are constant: only an improvement of two weeks on average over the past two hundred years as the comparison with Muirhead shows (see table). March will bring the wheatears, chiffchaffs and sandmartins, earliest of the swallows, but things really accelerate after the second week of April. Warblers, flycatchers, swallows, sandpipers and finally the swifts themselves will be arriving every day, while in the other direction the silent hordes of the winter migrants, the fieldfares and redwings, will be passing through on their way home to Scandinavia. Swans and geese too will be heading north. The pinkfeet return to the Borders to feast on the sprouting clover and young grass before leaving for Iceland. Sometimes the overlap is extraordinary. One year on May 10 I saw pinkfeet grazing in the fields by Greenlaw and willow warblers nesting at Hirsel, and in the autumn there

*Record of the arrival date in Berwickshire of some common summer migrants 1799–1976*

| Muirhead 1799–1887 | Earliest | Latest | Average |
|---|---|---|---|
| Swift | May 11 | May 30 | May 15 |
| Swallow | April 11 | May 11 | April 26 |
| House martin | April 21 | May 14 | May 3 |
| Sand martin | March 24 | May 15 | April 25 |
| Willow warbler | April 4 | May 9 | April 23 |
| Sandpiper | insufficient data | | |
| Redstart | April 24 | May 17 | May 2 |
| | | | |
| Douglas-Home 1918–1976 | | | |
| Swift | April 22 | May 12 | May 1 |
| Swallow | April 4 | April 29 | April 15 |
| House martin | April 12 | April 29 | April 18 |
| Sand martin | March 22 | April 20 | April 3 |
| Willow warbler | April 6 | April 22 | April 15 |
| Sandpiper | March 26 | April 21 | April 13 |
| Redstart | April 10 | May 6 | April 23 |

It should be remembered that techniques of observation were less sophisticated in Muirhead's day, which may account for a large part of the two week discrepancy between his dates and mine, though the pattern is surprisingly constant.

may still be late broods of housemartins wheeling the sky by the time of the first November pheasant shoots. No months are more exciting for birdwatchers than these two great seasonal passages, the best time for seeing rare birds: a great grey shrike in a flurry of hedgerow buntings and finches or, as at Hirsel, a graceful black tern, hovering and drifting like a big black swallow over the waters of Tweed. It is on the swallow, paradigm of all migrants, that I will end.

Swallows which nest with us have two main wintering quarters in South Africa – the largest concentration being just east of Cape Town and the second, almost as large, in the Durban area of Natal. It appears that most of the Cape birds migrate north to Europe by the west coast of Africa and the Straits of Gibraltar, and I have seen thousands in March flying low in a constant stream up the coastal belt north of Casablanca.

Those wintering in the Durban area fly north up the east coast of Africa then follow the Nile before filtering throughout Europe and Russia to east of the Ural mountains. These birds will return after breeding by the same route whereas our western birds mostly return to the Cape by way of the Alps and Italy joining up with the eastern birds round the Nile Delta. The post-breeding journeys are more leisurely than the spring migration and the birds suffer tremendous losses through trapping, netting and shooting in southern Europe and North Africa. Old birds tired after their breeding efforts and young as yet unversed in the arts of self-preservation are ruthlessly destroyed.

It is estimated that three hundred million small migratory birds, including many swallows are killed each autumn in Italy alone on their way to their winter quarters. Many thousands of European swallows are ringed each winter at the Cape and Durban ringing stations by means of mist nets and two of the latest results from recoveries show some interesting facts.

One ringed bird at the Cape was recovered in Georgia, Russia, thirty-four days later, a distance of over six thousand miles; showing a daily flying distance of nearly two hundred miles, while another ringed at Durban was recovered at Whitley Bay, Northumberland, twenty-seven days later having travelled about 250 miles each day.

These figures become all the more remarkable because the distances are measured from the place of departure to the point of destination and make no allowance for feeding flights, detours around mountain ranges or deserts, bad weather or being 'checked' on their first day of arrival.

Most of our swallows will be away from our shores by mid-October but several times I have seen a late swallow hawking flies in mid-November. European swallows only breed at the northern-most point of their migration and have never been known to breed again after their return to South Africa.

Some confusion has arisen on this score because there are several African swallows which can be confused with our European breeding birds by reason of their appearance and similar habits. The way of the swallow has always held its fascination for us. An old story was printed in Muirhead's *Birds of Berwickshire*:

'A man to ascertain where they [swallows] went to in winter caught one and placed around its neck a piece of parchment inscribed "Kimmerghame Mill, Berwickshire". It returned the following spring with the reply "River Nile, Egypt".'

## 14. | Flocks and colonies

In the winter and autumn most birds gather into flocks and forage together. Some species like starlings and various winter migrants such as geese and thrushes remain relatively segregated, others band together: waders on the foreshore, gulls on the lakes and reservoirs, finches, buntings and sparrows through the fields, tits, redpolls, wrens and treecreepers in the woods, joined according to weather and position by numerous other species of our resident birds. It is a poor time for birdwatching, the identifying songs and plumage of the breeding season having, in most cases, long since disappeared.

For most people rooks are perhaps the most famous congregational birds. At one point only a few years ago it was estimated that a winter roost of rooks on the adjoining farm to mine of Todrig numbered twenty thousand birds which was then the British record, but they did me no harm. Yet in the old days as soon as the helpless young rooks were out on the branches every man and boy was mustered to shoot them down. At Hirsel there were four rookeries. Every year we shot about three thousand, and every year there were more of the birds than ever. Now there are a few very small colonies, which we seldom shoot, and they never increase in numbers.

Rooks were also said to be ominous birds. In the last century there was a rookery near the castle at Douglas, and when my great-grandfather was fairly young he got irritated with their cawing and ordered the keepers to get rid of them. They shot as many as they could and eventually the remainder deserted the rookery, which had been vast – about three hundred nests at least. One day not long after this when shooting in the grounds he was rudely stopped by an old crone who bawled him out for banishing the rooks.

'You've done a terrible thing, a terrible thing shooting the rooks!' she quavered.

'Really? I couldn't stand their noise you know. Rather bored with them.'

'You wait. They'll be back the day you die!'

He was quite used to politics so he never thought any more about this invective until the time came when he was slipping away and suddenly, to his horror, all the rooks came cawing into the trees around Douglas Castle.

'God rooks!' he exclaimed and then, lost in thought, subsided into his pillows. 'That means I'm going to die today.' And he did.

Rooks of course are not the only birds which have aroused our suspicions. Wrens were persecuted once for some unknown reason, and the blood-curdling cries of water rails and the snores of barn owls can still frighten anyone out of their wits on a dark night, but thankfully we are now more rational by day, even if we do still doff caps to those villainous magpies.

Rooks and herons are not the only birds that nest in woodland colonies. It also happenes to a less noticeable degree with song-birds.

Before bird tours at Hirsel I chart some nests of the more obvious species and on this occasion I was looking for an example of a redpoll. I had a friend along to help and we started our search in a very likely looking wood of young Scotch firs and spruce, the trees ideally just getting the better of a jungle of brambles, gorse and willowherb. We began looking as gently as possible, one to each side of a ride which had been cut through the plantation, and were only a few feet beyond the gate when we both discovered nests. It was no more than a hundred yards to the other fence, so I suggested we continue and see how many we could find just dawdling along the side of the thicket. No sooner had we restarted than he called across to say that he had found another and so we went on, both of us in hotter and hotter competition until by the end we had clocked up a total of twenty-seven separate nests, some of them two to a tree. It can be imagined how many there must have been in the entire sixty acres of the plantation.

The great colony nesters are the seabirds. I have suffered every form of persecution visiting their large, discordant assemblies and never can imagine how one bird can recognise its clutch from all the others littering the ground roundabout. I have been dive-bombed by great skuas, scratched by terns, bitten by puffins, squirted with ineradicable and foul smelling ink by fulmars and covered with well aimed flak by all of them. No doubt these birds trust us literally to walk among them because of their un-familiarity with man, and it was a sad but inevitable betrayal when vandals wilfully destroyed six hundred eider nests on the Farne Isles, thus ensuring that all the rest of us now have to watch many of those priceless colonies from a zoolike distance.

It must also be said that numbers of birds together can be a pest.

Bullfinches which strip orchards of buds, pigeons which eat down winter greens, but most of all starlings, all arouse regular outbursts of public fury. I have long been of the opinion that there is no doubt birds can spread epidemic diseases like foot and mouth. Starlings I particularly suspect of being carriers as they migrate into Britain from the Continent and restlessly move in vast numbers round the countryside. I watched one epidemic of this disease move from East Anglia through to Hampshire entirely in accordance with starling movements, and the Northumberland outbreak of a decade ago, which almost led to the slaughter of the ancient, totally irreplaceable and, in the circumstances, blameless Chillingham herd of indigenous British cattle, was undoubtedly helped along far more by birds than animals or humans. There was even a decision to exterminate roedeer being considered while, as we stood in disinfected wellington boots or drove our cars through disinfectant sprays, herring gulls and carrion crows flew happily overhead from their latest feast on the unburied, contaminated carcases, their feet, beaks and even plumage carrying the virus wherever they chose.

My own wars have always been waged against house sparrows. To have outside aviaries as I do is inviting trouble, and I once killed four hundred in three days so that there would be a few crumbs left for the birds for whom the food was intended. Somehow the sparrows soon repaired their losses. This decimation was achieved with a sparrow trap. If you dip the whole contraption under water death follows instantly, but it was a rather beastly business nonetheless. So later I travelled the Borders with carloads of the birds, squawking their heads off and smelling like nothing on earth, releasing them to the care of my unsuspecting neighbours. I was only caught once.

'What in God's name are you doing Henry?'

'It's quite all right,' I said, continuing to unload the traps. 'They're like racing pigeons. I'm seeing if they'll get home before I do.' The sparrows went up in a great whirr.

Probably some of them did find their way back to pester me.

## Flocks and colonies

You cannot stop them. In a steading three miles away there used to be an albino, and with increasing regularity I noticed I was visited by an albino at home. Naturally I checked on the other steading when this bird was with me and found that its albino was missing. And that was how I came to realise just how far they were capable of travelling, even for such a casual meal. In a way they have their own charm but I am afraid that in the countryside, at least, I find them insufferable. They are unpleasant and they know it. The gentler birds – hedge sparrows, coal and marsh tits – stand no chance against their gangs. They will eat the eggs and even the young of other species but, apart from the occasional sparrow hawk, have no real enemies themselves except cats.

## 15. | Songs and recordings

In London I lived in a house with a garden in Hampstead. September 2, 1939, had been a lovely day but at dusk a thick mist closed in. The next morning I could sense that extraordinary feeling that those of us who had felt the rumble of war for so long would not have long to wait before the storm broke. I went down and opened the french windows to the garden and the dense mist came floating into the room. I turned on the wireless, but before it operated, very close by but invisible came the delicate, haunting song of a willow warbler from the complete silence outside. Almost immediately the sombre voice of Chamberlain announced that we were at war. Somehow I felt that while the willow warbler sang, one day there would be sunshine and peace again. About an hour later the sun broke through in all its September splendour and Alec and I spent the afternoon looking for chalk blues on the Downs.

Song is the glory of birds as much as colour and movement and my short sight has made me appreciate it all the more. Birds sing to protect their territories and to attract mates, but they also sing for pleasure and, like humans, some species and some individuals within species do it better than others. Francis Collinson, formerly C. B. Cochrane's master of music, is a friend of mine and he became most intrigued in the subject. He even transcribed one of my recordings of miscellaneous song into a 'Trio on Birdsong Themes' for flute, cello and clarinet, which was published and I believe successfully performed. In turn several species of bird can reproduce snatches of recognisable music. The best I ever heard at doing this was a cock blackbird, which I recorded outside the fisherman's hut above the Birgham Dub on Tweed singing to a rival in England on the other bank. I played its imitation to Francis and he identified it as the opening of Mendlesshon's 'Second Symphony'. He was amazed. It was note perfect and the purest rendering he said he had ever heard.

Many artists, Beethoven and Shakespeare not least, have been inspired by calls and songs of birds – by the cuckoo, the lark and the turtle (as the King James Version describes the turtle dove) and many others, but most of all by the nightingale. The nightingale is a warbler, and whether you prefer it to all other birds or not, it is difficult to imagine the prize going to some member other than one of the two great songster families, the warblers and thrushes. My list reads willow warbler first, blackbird second and the nightingale third.

Willow warblers sing the same phrase almost every half-minute of daylight from April to June. Some may call it a ditty, but for me the twenty seconds of its lovely cadence is finer than all the stronger voices it contends with. It sings in a minor key. In the major there is nothing more mellifluous than the song of the blackbird: a less ecstatic song than the redwing's, such a mouse of a bird in the winter when we see it but the most ardent singer of all the thrushes once it has returned to Scandinavia, more predictable than the harsher flights of the songthrush, but richer than both in melody and tone. As for the nightingale, it is hard to imagine anyone not choosing it as one of their three favourites. And then there are the calls of the curlew, the choruses of the pinkfeet, the strong voice of the tiny wren, the solitary autumn song of male robins, even the dipper's warble, so rarely audible above the rush of the waters. All just as powerfully evocative of landscapes and seasons, and all different.

Before the War I recorded numerous nightingales in the woods of the south of England. Only one has ever been identified in Scotland and if people hear a warbler singing through the night in the north it will undoubtedly be a black cap or a sedge warbler, both of which are also nightsingers and when in good voice do bear some resemblance to the nightingale. Years ago Beatrice Harrison made some famous recordings in which she enticed the bird to sing by playing her cello in the woods, but we found that almost any record played over the loudspeaker from the recording van goaded the local birds into action however dismal the weather. The same is true of most species in the breeding season when their territorial instincts are on edge. Chaffinches are the worst, being so numerous and aggressive. Over the years I suppose I have recorded more of them than of all other birds put together, not by deliberate intent but usually because they have taken it upon themselves to deliberately frustrate all my attempts to perpetuate the songs of rarer species. I have had my moments of revenge. One time in particular having had another meticulously en-gineered recording drowned out, we sat in the B.B.C. control car playing back the record while the offending chaffinch stamped furiously on the roof, under the impression that his own song was that of an aggressor to whom we had given political asylum. This fury is often self-engendered by the sight of their own reflection in the window of a house, and I have watched them battering at a pane for as much as half-an-hour before exhaustion has finally driven them off. Pied wagtails, great tits, even blackbirds will be similarly enticed. Ludwig Koch, one of the greatest authorities on the songs of birds, convinced himself that chaffinches had regional dialects as well as foreign tongues. Latest researches prove he may have been right!

Francis Collinson and I eventually did a series of programmes on 'Birds and Music'. One day he produced a lovely recording of the Glasgow Orpheus Choir singing an old folksong 'The Sweet Nightingale':

> 'Have you ever heard tell
> of the sweet nightingale
> who lived in the valley below
> who lived in the valley below?'

He played it, and from where I was in the studio I suggested we superimpose the live voice of a nightingale by transmitting both at the same time. It was incredible. The bird might have been part of the choir, its phrasing, rhythm and even volume were faultless. I have played the record of this dual recording many times since when short of words in a lecture, and always at the end strings of people have come forward to ask how they could obtain a copy. I have always had to disappoint them because it never crossed our minds to produce it as a commercial record. But I must hasten to add that not all my recording ventures were so successful.

Until recently the recording of birds was a very difficult operation, and in its infancy. No recordings, for instance, had been made of Scottish birds till I began with the Scottish B.B.C. in the War. There were two ways in which birds could be recorded: one was to position the microphone in a secluded place, and then go back to the recording van or hut and wait; the other was to take the microphone on a lead and stalk the bird until you were within range. Large birds could be picked up at remarkable distances but for the smaller species the microphone needed to be within eight feet for a worthwhile result. The microphones were extremely sensitive and often noises could be heard on disc that had been inaudible to me during the making of it. Everything could come between you and the particular voice you wanted – distant lorries, aeroplanes, wind, water, the calls of other birds, as well as the inevitable unforeseen hasards. In Dundock the acoustics are so good that even a whispered commentary delivered some feet from the mouthpiece sounded thunderous.

Shortly before the War we were doing a live broadcast, and as normal we switched into each mike to check that everything was relaying OK before going on the air. The mikes were set about the wood to pick up the calls of various different species but on this particular evening when we tuned into the garden warbler a breathless voice whispered:

'Darling, darling.' For a second I thought we had got a crossed line but the ensuing noises convinced me that this was much more serious. I made off at full gallop immediately. It was only a matter of minutes before we went live. The mike was dangling from the branch of a rhododendron bush and there on the ground three feet below it, when I pushed my head through the branches, was a loving couple stark naked.

'I'm frightfully sorry for interrupting like this but unless you are out of here within three minutes every word you say will be heard all over Britain,' I explained. There was a terrible commotion.

'Who the bloody hell are you?' demanded a puce face.

'Listen. I'm very sorry but there's a microphone there,' I gestured, 'and it's picking up every sound you make so unless you keep quiet or get out you'll be on the air for the next thirty minutes.' Without further persuasion they had gathered their clothes together and were sprinting off down the path. As they turned the corner his parting words echoed through the wood: 'This country's worse than bloody Hitler.'

These occasions just before going on the air were always nerve-wracking. Another time our programme was scheduled to follow Evensong on a Sunday evening. Bird song was thought to be soulful music and sufficiently pure to fulfil this task, and one weekend my boss Seymour de Lotbinière decided to sit in with me as I transmitted. We decided to record from his car. The rain thundered on the roof, a howling gale blew and there was not sight or sound of a bird. As usual just before we came on the air Stuart Hibbert did a voice test from London:

'We're now going over to a wood in Sussex for a programme of live bird songs, etc.'

'I simply must relieve nature,' I said to Seymour.

'You can't!' he exclaimed, horror-struck.

'I've got to. I simply must.'

'But what happens . . . for god's sake!'

'Don't flap. I don't want to go in a big way.'

'I should bloody well hope not. Hurry up.'

So I did. The broadcast was devoid of bird song. I improvised a few stories between the downpours from the trees overhead and the occasional 'caw' of a passing rook, and got through somehow.

'Well done,' said Seymour. 'It was an impossible situation. We should have cancelled,' (which I begged him to do before), 'but you handled it very well in the circumstances.'

However as the engineer approached from his hut we could see he was looking rather upset. I was fully prepared for it all to have been a failure.

'Did it go all right?' asked Seymour.

'Yes, beautifully,' said the engineers, still looking rather downcast, 'but I must apologise. I'm afraid after the voice test I forgot to cut you off so the whole of that conversation about Mr Home wanting to go to the lavatory went through.'

'Oh God!' gasped Seymour. 'This is perfectly frightful.'

Actually it was not quite that disastrous because it had only been received by the B.B.C. headquarters and the technical staff at Daventry, but it was quite bad enough for me. For weeks I received letters of condolence, telephone calls and internal memos as to the state of my internal health until I hardly dared set foot in the B.B.C. again.

If I had one piece of advice to give to anyone starting to birdwatch I would say: concentrate on sound, not sight. Sound is the only absolutely reliable guide. Frequently when one is driving around people say 'What was that!' as a bird flashes past. I ignore the question. Any answer would be hopelessly speculative. And, like all these things, the more you master the subject, the more enthralling it becomes. One of the oddest bird sounds is the 'drum' of the woodpeckers. How it is created remains unsolved and people have listened and looked for years. They have removed branches on which the bird has drummed and inspected their surfaces for beak marks and hammered them with various instruments to reproduce the noise, all to no conclusion. In the old days it was thought to be made by the impact of the beak on hollow wood, but since the branch is not always hollow and its bark shows no evidence of drilling, most of the experts now say it is an artificial sound created by the beak itself on the wood. I think it is a combination of the two: partly mechanical, but only possible through the amplification caused by the beak coming into contact with the wood. On the Continent woodpeckers have developed a habit of drumming on corrugated tin roofs. The sound produced is definitely corrugated, but the mystery of its amplification remains; a woodpecker at half-a-mile sounds as loud as a human being beating the roof at fifty yards. Obviously the bird can only brush the surface with its beak otherwise it would break its neck or have a splitting headache. Woodpeckers drum on favourite branches spaced at intervals throughout their roughly half-mile square territories, the noise acting both as a deterrent to other males and a rallying point for any unmatched female.

By relying on sound you can immediately know if a strange bird has arrived almost as soon as you enter a wood. It is not left to chance. If it is there it will voice its presence. All the oddities I have come across over my many years of birdwatching I have first heard, then seen. Redwings do not nest in England, so we are told, but when I visited my son Peregrine at his school near Richmond in Yorkshire, I heard its quite unmistakable song. Only extremely close observation would have persuaded me that I had seen a redwing at that time of year. And it was the same when I was credited with the first official record of the nuthatch in Scotland almost half-a-century before.

The nuthatch too has a loud song. Having become familiar with them down south I knew the call well, and the moment I heard it coming from the beeches up the valley of the Leet I had no doubt at all. It did not take long to see the bird, and for the remaining week or two I shared its lonely hopes as it called and waited for a mate that never arrived. The following year my excitement was no less intense when yet again I heard the familiar cry issuing from the same stand of trees, but sadly with the same lack of result. Obviously the bird had settled in and stayed throughout the preceding winter so all being well there was clearly no reason for it not to survive another year. I made plans, and the next spring when I heard it I was ready.

The idea was that a friend of mine, Guy Charteris, an inveterate egg-collector who lived in Oxfordshire where there were lots of nuthatches, should send me up some clutches which I would get hatched out in nesting boxes by unsuspecting great tits. A colony would be formed and my nuthatch would have a mate at last. It was a complicated exercise because the eggs had to be kept to a certain temperature if they were not to addle on the journey, and in those pre-motorway days that took a lot of working out with train timetables to achieve. In the end I fell off a horse and the whole plan had to be abandoned.

Luckily this did not happen before I had the nuthatch's identity officially confirmed. News had reached the Misses Baxter and Rintoul from Edinburgh, authors of 'The Birds of Scotland' and the most revered Scottish experts of the day. They asked if they could be shown the bird, and duly arrived one spring morning in a chauffeur driven car to be conducted solemnly to the spot where, inevitably, we heard nothing. After a frustrating interval for lunch with my parents, we toured the grounds again but there was still no sign of the bird. The two old ladies were due to leave within the hour. I dashed out for a last desperate search and as I did so heard the well-known voice coming, loud and clear from the garden. 'Quick!' I ordered the exhausted ladies who were just settling down to a restorative cup of tea with my parents, and game to the last they followed me to where the cheeky bird was bursting with pent up song only a short distance from the house. 'Nuthatch', they confirmed in unison. That was the last spring we heard him.

Jack Vincent told me of a time he was travelling slowly through Natal in a train when suddenly he heard a song that was unknown to him coming from the Bush. He pulled the communication cord, and when the engine finally lurched to a stop, persuaded the driver to back down the mile or so of the track to where he had first heard the call. The bird was still singing, and that is how Vincent's warbler was discovered.

16. | *Nests and bird watching*

One night Alec telephoned me at 10 o'clock, so I knew it must be a matter of the utmost urgency. Possibly something to do with the Russians. 'I haven't got much time,' he began. 'How many feathers are there in a long-tailed tit's nest?'

'I think the record is three thousand, three hundred and eighty-three, but if you'll hold a couple of minutes I'll check.'

'I'm not interested in the odd hundreds. If I say three thousand that is all I need.'

'I suppose you're putting that in your Memoirs!'

'Yes, I am actually. Goodnight.'

And sure enough when his Memoirs appeared there on page 13 was this vital piece of information, because of course it is one of the most extraordinary of all bird statistics. The nest is an oval about twice the size of a swan's egg with an entrance hole in the top quarter. It is bound to, not supported by, the branches, especially of oak trees, and sometimes of tree trunks – the hole facing out and the outside heavily decorated with lichen, which makes it extremely difficult to see against the normally lichened backgrounds. It is fascinating to watch the birds building these remarkable edifices, the female staying inside the shell padding and cementing while the little male sits patiently ready to deliver the latest feather when she next pops out her head. The entire interior is gradually cushioned in this way right to the lip of the entrance for a depth of one inch. Fifty per cent of these feathers are from woodpigeons, the others a miscellany, often gathered from corpses. Each feather is picked individually and the amazing energy of the birds can be gleaned from the fact that the operation takes no more than three days to complete from start to finish.

When the female is sitting her tail sticks out of the hole like a twig, the reverse of a bird's normal position. They begin breeding as early as February, the clutches numbering eight to ten eggs with the ensuing squash sometimes causing bursts which leave the mother sitting in what looks like a chaffinch nest. Two broods are usually raised per season, each in a new nest. The endearing devotion of the parents is matched by the young birds which stay in the vicinity, flocking together as an enormous family when the breeding season is finished. Pairs will seldom nest closer than thirty yards of each other but never appear to have territorial disputes. By nature very gentle, they nevertheless instinctively keep their distance.

The best time to watch birds, is of course, during the nesting season when their plumage is at its most identifiable and their breeding preoccupations make them so easy to approach. And, in my experience, the nesting of long-tailed tits is the most rewarding to study.

As children we were trained never to touch a nest and never to search for nests, but to sit down, listen and look. This is the only way to discover the whereabouts of the more secretive and delicate builders, and also, having pinpointed their position by the movements of the birds, of ultimately seeing their nests, which are usually camouflaged from the attentions of a casual glance. Birds use much the same places, often exactly the same holes or branches for generations, so that once the initial discovery has been made the birdwatcher can often determine the likely sites the following season with what looks like remarkable prescience. I can remember countless times at Hirsel when somebody has wanted to see the nest of a bird I had not considered as worth inclusion in the day's schedule – a linnet or redpoll for instance – and I have been able to find one instantly by this method. Birdnesting is as absorbing and taxing a pleasure as fishing – in both pastimes patience is refined to an art.

The beauty and construction of nests is a study in itself. The gold crest makes a wonderful example: half the size of a tennis ball in moss and feathers, and slung with cobwebs to hang like a hammock from under the tip of a branch. In spring one comes fluttering against my windows collecting cobwebs from the sheltered corners of the panes. At Hirsel there is a long-established site at the end of the lower branches of an old yew. I have seen the whole tree thrashing frantically in an April storm but never once has the wind broken the silk sling of the nest, while the heavier constructions of other birds are frequently dumped by a gale: thrushes and blackbirds regularly, woodpigeons, rooks and all the prop and tether builders. The only other European bird to hang its nest is the golden oriole, which weaves its sling from grass and dresses the bowl with oak leaves – in 1973 a schoolboy discovered an empty one near Kelso. Nobody saw the great rarities which must have made it. Gold crests usually build in the branches of mature yews, spruces, cedars and ornamental conifers. but once in Sussex I discovered their treasure in a knee-high, tightly clipped box hedge which surrounded a formal rose garden.

Long-taileds, gold crests, orioles are all builders of superbly ornate nests, the hawfinch builds the flimsiest I know, a frail net of apparently randomly scattered twigs, like a miniature woodpigeon's through which the eggs are clearly visible from below.

When the house at Hirsel was being renovated in the early 'sixties, the workmen used to take their meals under the same small thorn tree every day, and they reported to me that there was a bird like a parrot nesting over their heads. Hawfinches are rare and secretive birds, but at Hirsel I have since discovered that they too return season after season to this tree. Many birds patch up the same nest season after season, ravens most spectacularly of all. Some of their constructions are ten feet deep at least and may date back hundreds of years.

It is always easy to check if an old nest is being used because it will soon reveal tell-tale evidence of reoccupation. If a kingfisher is back the stench and spill of its white droppings at the entrance will be warning enough, and a sprinkling of fresh wood chips at the foot of a tree will disclose the bore marks of a woodpecker. Peculiarly birds nesting near water never make any allowance for a rise, however marginal, in the water level. Perhaps to compensate for such losses waterhens tend to have four broods in a season, but it applies just as much to dippers, kingfishers, ducks and waders. As with the tree-nesting mallard there are intelligent exceptions. I have found kingfishers nesting in a bank sixty feet above Tweed, and one day when I was watching a greater spotted woodpecker chiselling out a hole in one of Dundock's high Scots firs I saw a waterhen fly into the top of a tall rhododendron bush. It did not reappear so I investigated and discovered it sitting in an old pigeon's nest. Such use of abandoned sites by a bird of another family the following year is not uncommon. The cup of a swallow in a garden shed may first form the core of the wren's frizzy nest and then of the all enveloping cone of a wasp's.

I have always marvelled at the lovely, grey whorled dome of the wasp's nest, all made from wood chewed into pulp by the queen whose abode it becomes through the winter after the swarm has died. Given the chance they will often build these beautiful edifices against a wall and ceiling inside a house, quite securely and with no risk of harm to anyone: they used to build in the bedroom of my present house. The only risk is if the queen hibernates elsewhere. In spring you should always shake out any receptacle left standing over winter before using it, shoes most obviously. My housemaster Mr Wells told me of an occasion when he was fielding at slip in the opening match of the cricket season at Lords and the great C. B. Fry came to the crease. He took guard and then 'uttered a dweadful scweam, like a woman and fell withing to the gwound. Dweadful, dweadful. There was a hibernating queen in his pwotector.'

The cuckoo's habit of laying its eggs in other birds' nests is undoubtedly the most eccentric breeding trait of any bird. Edgar Chance, who was almost a cuckoo himself, knew of one female which had planted twenty-seven eggs in this way but the average is much less. At Hirsel there was a female that used to sit on a stone balustrade just below the window, so that one had a very good view of her even without field-glasses. For several years a pair of hedge sparrows used to use a low juniper bush about twenty feet from where the cuckoo normally perched, and the cuckoo always deposited her egg with them. This particular spring the hedge sparrows were still building when the cuckoo arrived. The cuckoo sat it out for a couple of days throwing envious looks at the bush and then one morning, as I was watching, she swooped down, emerged a second later without a hedge sparrow's egg in her beak, and flew off. This was most puzzling. Normally the cuckoo removes one egg and replaces it with one of its own. I investigated immediately and found that the hedge sparrow's nest had not been completed: they were putting the finishing touches to it and the cuckoo's egg was the first to have been laid. In my experience this was unique. Later the female hedge sparrow laid her clutch around it and the baby cuckoo levered these out of the nest in its own time.

Other birds build surplus nests. Pied flycatchers do this and, most elaborately, wrens. The male wren will build as many as four of his bushy, domed balls without lining them, and the female will show her preference by carrying in a feather with which to begin this final operation. But the unused nests are not necessarily wasted. Adult wrens may use them as winter roosts. Another peculiar feature of birds which one discovers over the years is the way in which they will sometimes disregard odd proximities or choose odd places. Some I have mentioned, but there have been many others: different species nesting on top of each other or back to back, quite unperturbed. I have seen jackdaws use the base of an extra large rook nest, despite all the commotion over their heads, and a carrion crow near Greenlaw even had the effrontery to nest in one of the jumps used by Freddie, the great steeplechaser who was runner-up so many times in the Grand National.

Crows and gulls are the muggers of bird society, and like most of the criminal classes they are not short of character, but the jackdaw is the most incorrigible of the gang. In my youth I pilfered hundreds of their nests, partly for their eggs which are as delicious as a plover's, partly to reduce their numbers and mostly for fun, and I soon discovered that they had as many oddities in them as a museum. There were extraordinary things: huge sheets of paper, cigarette cards and packets, silver foil, bottle tops, anything in fact that had caught their eye. The famous legend of how a jackdaw went off with the ring of the Cardinal of Rheims is not unlikely at all. Muirhead tells the story of a frightful scene which took place in his time, when some old boy having laboriously made out his will, wandered out of the room to get a drink, only to find the precious document missing on his return. There was a terrible row, and he fell out with all his relations by accusing each of them in turn of having stolen it. A few weeks later one of his sons, searching the park trees just like I used to do, found the will spread below five jackdaw eggs. One of the birds must have flown down the chimney while the man was out and made off through the window with this eye-catching piece of paper.

Rooks are always thought the most blameless of the crows and although this may be true, they are also bigger thieves than we like to think, particularly of pheasant and partridge eggs in a bare late spring when the clutches have been laid before the grass has grown. I have bantams in a run in a paddock, and one week something began to rob their eggs. I thought it must be carrion crows, so I poisoned three eggs and put them on top of the aviary; within two hours two of them had gone and there were a dozen rooks lying stone-dead within thirty yards.

But the worst of the crows is the carrion. A carrion will not just discover a partridge nest, it will take a careful inventory of all the partridge (and other) nests in its half-mile territory and having memorised their whereabouts will only rob them when a bird has laid a full clutch. Carrions can withstand any amount of urban pollution and are found everywhere except where they have been replaced by their cousins, the grey-mantled hooded crow. On the east of Scotland all crows are called 'hoodies' but in fact there is a very clear diagonal line running from Perth through Lanark, to the west of which you have the hooded and to the east the carrion. The width of interbreeding along the length of this line is about fifteen miles, and it is a measure of the birds' basic similarity that about one in five of both types of crow will mate with its opposite, though the results of such crosses are usually distinctive of one bird or the other.

Crows and the other egg thieves are aided and abetted by ourselves. Hedgerow birds like the yellow hammers, white-throats and partridges have had their habitat uprooted or laid bare by weedkiller and, these days, the ravages of electric cutters. Ground nesters are caught by the rapid harvesting of wet grass for sileage and the efficiency of garden mowers, especially that terror of warblers, the flymo. Huge soft wood plantations – useless for all birds except pigeons once the trees are ten years old – have taken the place of the rough ground of the wheaters and chats, and the varied timber of the old estates has been felled to make way for cash crops and quicker yields. Drainage has dried out our marshes, even the fens, and basic to it all is the water pollution which we now bear as a necessary evil of modern existence. All this has gone hand in hand with a great increase in our knowledge and interest in birds.

Happily at Hirsel the land has been maintained, keepered and timbered and is as uncontaminated as present life permits, and to this sanctuary come more and more birdwatchers every year. The grounds are open to the public free as they have always been, and my niece Caroline has mapped out a series of walks which reveal the place to its best advantage. I have had the privilege of welcoming many pre-arranged tours and conducting them round. Incidents abound: two noted Dutch authorities swore they heard reed warblers by the Lake and the American Audubon Society discovered Alec semi-nude in the rose garden. Ninety-nine species have now been officially recorded to have bred and one hundred and ninety-three have been seen. As detection improves the list increases. In 1974 yellow wagtails rare to the area and always assumed to be common because of their similarity to the misnamed grey wagtail, were discovered by a bird tour nesting by Tweed in a field of barley. It is always an exciting time.

On the Continent there is a very handsome woodpecker about the size and colouring of a crow but with a magnificent shock of red crest on its head, which alas we never get in this country: the black woodpecker. Some years ago it was reported to have been seen by an eminent bird authority 'walking' across the road near Carham on the south bank of Tweed, presumably having struck a telegraph wire. It was June and just conceivable, so I went off to prospect the nearest wood, a bank of trees overlooking the water. After searching high and low I idly scanned the shingle by the river for nesting waders and suddenly caught my breath because in the water beyond there was a resplendent drake Barrow's goldeneye in full breeding plumage. This was an unbelievable coincidence because if a black woodpecker has never been seen in Scotland, a Barrow's goldeneye has hardly ever been reported in Britain. Even an ordinary goldeneye was rare enough at that time of year. All thought of anything so mundane as a black woodpecker went by the board as I scrambled down to get a better view. Once at the water's edge however it became quite clear that it was indeed an ordinary goldeneye and, since it allowed me to approach without taking off, obviously a pricked bird from the previous winter's shooting. Interrogation later suggested that the black woodpecker, unlikely to be seen walking across a road at the best of times, was nothing more than a waterhen. A typical birdwatching, birdnesting day!

## 17. | *Aviaries and pets*

I do not remember my first pet bird but there have been a great
many since and now I could not exist without them. Most birds
are very dependent on us for their well-being, far more so than
perhaps we realise – even one properly maintained bird-table will
make a great difference to the strength and numbers of a local
population. If they are fed however it is best continued throughout the year not, as many people seem to think, simply when
there is snow on the ground: a string or two of peanuts through
the summer, more in the winter and always, just as importantly,
grit and water. There is a theory that no bird should be fed
artificially once the young have been hatched because the nestlings
will be unable to digest the food. I do not think this is true, but it
is not necessary to feed them heavily at high summer in any case.
Regular feeding will ensure that when the bad weather does come
all your local birds will know where to get food at once. If you
feed them only in hard weather it may take some time for the

news to spread and therefore you will not see all the birds you should. Worst of all is to feed them in and then stop either out of callous neglect or because you have had to go away. The birds may waste valuable hours in the expectation of their routine meal and not have sufficient energy as a result to survive the cold of another night.

Tits are the most adaptable of our garden birds. Their formidable beaks afford them a better chance of survival than is usual among other birds of their size and they use them most inventively. Probably the most notorious of these inventions is the way in which blue tits have learned to get at the cream in the necks of milk bottles by pecking through the tinfoil caps. This was a discovery of London blue tits but is now practised by the continental birds to an equal degree, presumably introduced by London migrants. When the habit first came to the notice of ornithologists experiments were made to see how the birds determined where the cream was. The differently coloured bottle caps were interchanged, whitewash substituted for milk and so on, but except for an occasional pause for thought the blue tits continued to be correct. This suggests that they were guided by smell. Blue and great tits will always come to fat, half cocoa nuts, breadcrumbs and, most entertainingly for watching purposes, unshelled peanuts threaded on a string left to dangle.

Great tits are the biggest of all the species and use their size to dominate the rest. They are bullies, carnivores and even predators, sometimes evicting the blue from nesting sites, eating the eggs and, if they are hunting in a pack, the young as well. Their meat eating tendencies are usually confined to the flecks sticking to fat scraps, but in the wild they are sometimes to be seen picking carcases. Both birds are very fond of nesting boxes and will otherwise test the nesting capacity of a building to the full, exploring the possibilities of every crack, crevice and pipe. I once found great tits nesting down a $3\frac{1}{2}$-foot section of narrow gauge piping that had been left leaning against a wall. After they had left I checked to see where the nest had been and found it placed on the ground at the very bottom. How the young had wormed their way up that slippery sheer wall I shall never know.

In pre-war editions of Jourdain's *Birds of Britain*, the bible of birdwatchers at that time, Bernard Tucker had decreed that there were no marsh tits in Scotland. As I knew of at least a dozen pairs at Hirsel alone, I wrote to the old boy and suggested that the entry be corrected. On receipt of my letter he despatched Bruce Campbell from Oxford to see what I was talking about: 'Bernard's having fits at your suggestion', he reported on arrival. But I showed him the birds and he went south to deliver the *coup de grâce*. I heard nothing further from Tucker, but in the next edition of the book I was gratified to see that 'Unknown in Scotland' had been amended to read 'Unknown in Scotland except infrequently in Berwickshire'. They are even more numerous in the south-eastern Lowlands today than they were then.

Nesting-boxes are the best way of ensuring good views of birds, and also of increasing the numbers of the species you prefer. I have done this most successfully with swifts and pied flycatchers, but boxes have worked well with numerous others, and they are very easy to make and install. One of my most successful experiments was with spotted flycatchers. Half a cocoa-nut shell wedged securely among the branches of a creeper has attracted as many as twenty pairs to a single garden wall at Hirsel. The only important thing to remember is to bore drainage holes to prevent the cup becoming waterlogged. Bigger birds like tawny owls are equally easy to attract in conifer woods. Where I have failed is in not preventing northern migrants like the goldeneye and, on another occasion, bramblings from leaving.

Nesting boxes and bird-tables are not the only way of attracting birds. If you have a garden you can also plant intelligently. Sunflowers are probably the most decorative and nutritious enticements for seedeaters like finches; and catoneasters, rowans, yews and other berry fruiting trees will keep thrushes happy through the winter. I have also discovered how easily injured wild birds adapt to care and captivity.

## Aviaries and pets

Some of the wildest birds seem the most amenable. I once took in that shyest of all the garden birds, a hawfinch, with a sprained wing. It was immediately trusting and had a colossal appetite. I fed it handfuls of yewberries and acorns which it stripped and cracked in seconds – bang, bang, bang – and then sang a very sweet almost inaudible song for more. It was the easiest bird imaginable but too insatiable, so after a time, having to return to the army, I left the cage and windows open: out it hopped, preened and was gone.

The late Mr Street, who ran a wonderful pet-shop in Kelso for many years, had a winged female kestrel in a cage in his window. It attracted the attention of a wild mate which, to the astonishment of the customers, used to swoop in and out of the shop at will, Mr Street's door always being open. He demonstrated the variety of birds that can be kept happily in captivity, and the way in which they should be kept, better than anyone I have known. Apart from maintaining open shop for the town kestrel, he had a whole attic devoted to various types of wildlife at his home. You had to enter this sanctuary up a ladder. Once when I went round he called down that I should watch out for my head because he had a new guest. I did not pay much attention but as soon as I poked my nose through the hatch a ferocious old cock pheasant came at me like a whirlwind. I only just retreated in time. Eventually he had to rescue me by gathering up the bird until I was on my feet. It was as docile as a lamb with him. There in his sunlit attic, with bees coming through the open skylight to two hives in the corner, was his latest crop of the halt and lame brought to him, as was the custom, from every point of the neighbourhood. Alas he died in the autumn of 1976 and his petshop in Bridge Street has long since been given over to new construction.

At home I have two outside aviaries both twenty feet square with a Norwegian type of converted summer-house at one end. They enclose a few bushes and a shallow concrete pond in which the birds drink and bathe. The first problem was how to keep out rats. Underground concrete was no good because it cracks and also prevents the grass from growing. I have found that two layers of wire mesh laid under the turf is the best solution. The sides of the aviary are also blocked off to a height of two feet with asbestos, chiefly to prevent the young Chinese painted quail from escaping through even the smallest netting, being no larger than a bee. Young quails are also suicidal with regard to water. You have to pull out the plug from the basin otherwise the whole lot will be drowned within minutes. Caging a bird is not cruel. As long as it has regular food, water and is living in a warm enough temperature it will be happy, more or less regardless of the size of its cage or aviary. It is rarely too warm for birds but they hate cold and most foreign species should be brought indoors through the winter. In hard weather almost any bird prefers to be cooped up and warm than free and cold. In winter too aviaries inevitably fill up with mice. This does not disturb the birds but is a drain on food.

The easiest birds to breed in aviaries – some of them like African finches are almost too easy (one pair might raise twenty young in a season) – are finches (zebra, African, Bengalese, green singing and various canaries), cordon bleus, waxbills and doves. The diamond dove, the second smallest in the world, is a special favourite of mine and happily settles down indoors in a 3 × 2 foot cage for the winter. Directly the weather warms up and the various birds are in breeding condition they go back into my outside aviaries to nest.

Many birds are very vicious at this time both in captivity and the wild. Diamond doves may kill their young if they are not moved out after the third week, and males of all pigeon species should never be left alone together in a confined space. That symbol of Christmas good cheer the robin redbreast is probably the most viciously protective of its territorial rights, the males expelling the young and females after the breeding season, again killing those obstinate or stupid enough not to leave. My bigger birds roam free in the orchard but despite the space are just as liable to violence. Turkeys are famous for it and recently I lost a rare and expensive bird called a Hume's pheasant when the cock killed the hen, but the worst of the ornamental pheasants is the silver. Never take children near them, they are liable to leap up like fighting cocks without provocation and are quite capable of blinding an eye with a strike from their spurred legs.

The other advantage of outdoor aviaries is that they make wonderful hospitals for damaged wild birds. You can splint a wing or leg with a matchstick and elastoplast and put the injured bird in there along with the healthy residents to recover. The injury will normally have cleared up in a couple of weeks and these wild birds can then be released. I had a waterhen with a permanently damaged wing which lived for seven years and a peewit, later transferred to Edinburgh Zoo, which survived even longer.

But the easiest and most entertaining of all my birds was an Indian hill mynah. Here, as in life, I shall give the last word to 'Gluck', who lived with me for sixteen years. Gluck was a constant source of interest and amusement. On one occasion a very proper old lady from Edinburgh wanted me to write a book for her. We were reviewing one of her publications on the sofa with me standing over her when Gluck gave one of his special wolf whistles.

'Major! How dare you!' she exclaimed, clapping the volume shut and almost removing my nose.

'It wasn't me I assure you. It was the bird.'

'Well, if it was the bird it certainly isn't doing it now.'

This was quite true. I tried to make Gluck demonstrate his whistle again but he would not utter. The lady was most unconvinced. We resumed, and at an even more inappropriate moment the wretched bird ditched me again – this time for good.

## 18. | Finale

The first time that I was ever aware of pollution was when I went to the War Office in 1938 and heard talk of gas masks. Now familiarity has made us contemptuous of pollution as a subject, but it is chemical poisoning that divides the world of my youth from my old age, my knowledge of birds from that of Muirhead. In only thirty years I would estimate that the number of songbirds at Hirsel has dropped by a third from this one cause alone and although, as we have seen, the population of some birds has increased, most other species are now in decline to some degree. Muirhead saw a few species making way for others, but what his reaction would have been to discover whole species threatened with ultimate extinction can only be guessed at. Perhaps like the rest of us he would have wondered how it was possible for us to have made such a mess in such a short time.

Yet despite all this we can congratulate ourselves on our awareness of the problem and the success of some of our conservation policies. It is true, for instance, that in Britain we have government-controlled agrochemical schemes like the Pesticide Safety Precautions and the Agricultural Chemicals Approval to ensure that wild life is protected as far as possible from chemical poisoning; and certainly Dieldrin, Aldrin and other related chlorinated hydrocarbons have now been withdrawn from the market. I am told that only a few mercurial based seed-dressings remain that could have any detrimental effect on wildlife at all and that the restrictions on their use become more rigorous all the time, but I also know that such laws are impossible to enforce and that once a product has been manufactured the manufacturer will sell it somewhere, rather than make a loss. What is difficult to market here will be sold in Europe or Africa and the effect on our birds, many of our species travelling between the two, will be just the same in the long run as if we had never had a ban at all. The survival of birds is something that can finally only be guaranteed by obedience to strict international sanctions which, as we all know, nobody has the right to impose and which, therefore, can be disobeyed with complete impunity.

In any case the success of our good intentions can always be checked by the evidence of the facts. I read of catastrophic oil leaks, I pick up scores of dead rooks and woodpigeons in spring and see the weed on the river beds waving like fields of barley. Worst of all I have witnessed the same things beginning to happen in Africa.

The oxpecker was one of the most common and attractive of South African birds. They feed principally on the ticks in animal hides. The authorities insisted on the inoculation of all cattle and the ticks died. By 1975 almost all the oxpeckers had vanished, except in the dwindling bush. What is true of the oxpecker is no less true of all the African species now threatened with the introduction of chemicals and technology on a European scale. And yet in Europe there are still countries, Italy most heinously, where small migratory birds are slaughtered for food in colossal numbers.

For years I had complained about this without much support but in 1975 an article I wrote in *The Times* prompted the following reply from the Komitee Gegen den Vogelmord EV of Germany:

'Regarding only one point, a little additional remark might be permitted to us, since it is of considerable importance. Not 160 millions of small migratory birds as mentioned in your article but very many more, including swallows, are killed each year only in Italy. Documented figures are speaking about more than 300 millions of birds remaining each year victims of bird slaughter in Italy.

As a very alarming matter of fact, only one in six swallows is still returning from the south to breeding grounds in northern Europe and ever since eight years breedings and all efforts on bird protection have proved not being sufficient to avoid a considerable decrease of many species of birds. This presents a big problem which should be taken in serious consideration by everyone.'

The E.E.C., thanks chiefly to the efforts of Sir Christopher Soames, has now endorsed a comprehensive decree of bird protection throughout the member countries, which of course include Italy, but although this is a step forward it is difficult to see how it can be enforced any more successfully than similar international measures to combat pollution.

When things were looking bleak for the Western Powers in the last War, Field Marshal Alanbroke took a short leave to this country. He did not attend conferences at the War Office nor with the War Cabinet. He retired to a wood in southern England and watched and filmed a pair of nesting hobbies.

I have derived the same comfort and satisfaction from watching birds, and so have more and more people throughout my life as our world has become increasingly troubled and dangerous. I hope this book conveys something of that satisfaction, the incredible interest and beauty of the natural world which we know to be in danger unless we consider the plight we and it are in. The world of birds may not be as efficient as the technical world of man, but it is an older, more lovely and, I think, a more peaceful place.